ART DECO SCAPES

THE ART OF DISPLAYING YESTERDAY TODAY

ABRAHAM AND WALLACE

This book is dedicated to my Father, a military man and accomplished landscape painter, from whom I gained my passion for composition, and to my Mother, from whom I inherited a love of style and probably an appreciation of chrome, owing to her well known hatred of having to polish silver.

ART

GRAHAM ABRAHAM
MICHAEL WALLACE

DECOSCAPES

THE ART OF DISPLAYING YESTERDAY TODAY

A GUIDE TO THE GROUPING AND DISPLAY OF YOUR TWENTIETH CENTURY COLLECTABLES TO THEIR MAXIMUM ADVANTAGE FOR THE INTERIORS OF TODAY

SCHIFFER PUBLISHING LTD.
4880 LOWER VALLEY ROAD, RT. 372
ATGLEN, PENNSYLVANIA 19310 USA

ART DECOSCAPES

THE ART OF DISPLAYING YESTERDAY TODAY

Library of Congress Control Number: 2006935532

Designed by Graham Abraham and Michael Wallace
Type set in Futura ICG Lt, Futura BT Book Italic, Kabel Book and Premier Lightline

ISBN: 978-0-7643-2677-6
Printed in China

Published by Schiffer Publishing Ltd.
4880 Lower Valley Road
Atglen, PA 19310
Phone: (610) 593-1777; Fax: (610) 593-2002
E-mail: Info@schifferbooks.com

mative years crawling under market stalls looking for treasure for me, and Wayne Nakamura, Michael's Digital Mentor. Our team of tried and true specialists; Jeffrey Golde (He can fix anything), Arline and Alan Sharpe (Model and cabinet making), Happy and Cecil (Chromers extraordinaire), Brent Bayley (Horologist), Murray Macklin (The lamp doctor), Liz Hunt (Framing and gilding), Linton Glass, Joe the Sandblaster, Greg Woods (Ceramic restoration), Fred and Judy Mooij (Upholstery), Aristocrat Lighting, (Lamp shades), Malcolm Telford, (Furniture restoration), Tony Trevor (Furniture restoration), Chris Montgomery, (Glass restoration) and Tony and Lance Simpson (Who keep the doors open and the lights on at The Decollect Gallery). Our fellow Antique dealers in the area; Christopher Stuart, Smith Creek Antiques, Lee Caswell, Blaise Gaetz, Kendra Simmons, Susan who lent us items from their wonderful collections. Michael Vuksta and Rich Lane, Debbie and John Doherty, Shirley and Adrian Hanick and Brian King, who let us photograph their beautiful houses, Shelley Wickabrod and Joy and Gary Graham for information, Beth Thomson, for typing, Cobourg Digital, for digital proofs, John Nicol, for being the English connection, Robert Josephy, for design inspiration. Gary at The Beamish, Julie, Paul et. al. at Zest, for providing end of day sustenance, Nancy and Peter ("Where's my captions") Schiffer, for having the faith, our fabulous editor, Donna Baker (She who must be obeyed), all the designers both known and unknown who produced these wonderful objects in the first place. And last, but by no means least, You, The Reader, for buying our book. Please tell two friends and they'll tell two friends and they'll tell two friends and...

A R T D E C O

SCAPES

THE INTRODUCTION

THE CAPRICIOUS chronology of my personal collecting history all began innocently enough as a young child in the U.K. with model soldiers, military badges, war souvenirs, vintage edged weapons, early blues records, Victoriana, early advertising, fair isle sweaters, vintage leather jackets and art nouveau. Finally, in my early adulthood, my collecting culminated and remains firmly anchored in Art Deco.

Upon examination, the astute reader most probably will detect a distinct departure occurring between that of 'vintage edged weapons' and 'early blues records'. This, without doubt, manifested itself, when, much to my family's ill-concealed chagrin, I opted to enter Art College rather than pursue a career in the military.

Thus I found myself for the past thirty plus years somewhat successfully stumbling about the world working in the dubious and 'most fun that you can have with your clothes on' field of international advertising.

However, it is now, with a definite sense of pride and emancipation, that I can divulge that I have led a secret existence. A delightfully clandestine life that necessitated rising at unholy hours to haunt the antique shops and markets of whichever godforsaken city, town, village or hamlet in whatever corner of the world that I found myself in the search for my adored Art Deco.

It was an unrelenting dependence, an obsession that required me having heard the closing of the door as the bellhop left (after showing me the location of the trouser press, the coffee filters, the four kinds of conditioner in the shower, and the over priced mini bar) to bolt to the drawer containing the Bible and local phone directories. Forsaking the former, I would frantically grab the yellow pages in a desperate attempt to locate the antique district (to a true collector, just one shop can be rationalized to count as an 'antique district'). While fellow members of the creative department and film crew were still wisely tucked up in their beds sleeping and the account people were discussing the merits of the marketing strategy and munching on their muesli in the coffee shop, I, the creative director, tiptoed undetected out of the hotel. Moments later I could be found with a sumptuously greasy sausage on a bun clutched in hand, hovering in front of a market stall, joyfully haggling in acquiring my first Art Deco fix of the day.

Upon reluctantly returning to the hotel, and not wishing to endure the excruciating, "What! You paid how much! My grandmother/mother/aunt had one of those and we threw it out!" chastisements from my colleagues, I would stealthily sneak up to my room. There I would gleefully unpack my Art Deco treasures from crumpled newspapers and begin the process of bringing some individuality to the 'best surprise is no surprise' hotel room. Carefully I went to work, artfully displaying my finds grouped on the frightful faux wood credenza. This was the genesis of *Art Decoscapes*. But back then, save for the eyes of the hotel maid, mine was a singular and unshared indulgence. I cheerfully admit and indeed embrace the fact that in all probability I am an Art Deco addict. (With no intention whatsoever of changing, my willingness to twelve step is only if those twelve steps involve my own two feet and bring me closer to the proximity of a new and potentially prized purchase.)

I am telling this to you, my fellow collectors, because, as you well know, this is what collecting usually is, a solitary, oft unappreciated by others, secluded pleasure. I feel, however, that I can now reveal to you, that it need not be that way anymore. With the aid of this book it will be possible to display those beautiful bits and not only will these items be freed and look fabulous but outsiders may understand that there could be a vestige of merit in your magnificent obsession.

"Oh sure," I hear your inner skeptic collector voice argue, "Nobody can appreciate the beauty of a Number 4 first patent 'whatever' with original slot screws and an uncracked green Bakelite finial, in the same way that I do, save perhaps for another collector of Number 4 patent 'whatevers' with original slot screws and uncracked green Bakelite finials".

Perhaps not, but others may be able to respect and admire that same 'whatever' in a whole different way when it is properly displayed and grouped together with similar 'whatevers' from the Art Deco period that show the same design, color or functional attributes. The key to this miraculous attitudinal transformation is HOW you group and display your 'whatevers'.

Department stores have known this for years, and it is not altogether surprising that Macy's of New York (R. H. Macy and Co.) and their famous flair for display is credited with successfully presenting and in turn selling the concept of the modern movement in industrial design to the American people in its *Exposi-*

tion of Art In Trade in 1927.

This book will show you how it is possible to arrange pieces from your collection, whether that assemblage be large or small, and to show them off to their best advantage. In the first part you will learn the various ways to group a number of items and why in these groupings, it is nearly always good to be odd. You will discover the success of the Magnificent Seven, why five, not four of a kind, is a winner, and why three is seldom a crowd; furthermore you will be introduced to the "rule" and enchanting sure-fire success of the chrome triangle.

Moreover, and even perhaps more importantly, I hope that this work will inspire new collectors — those who are taking their first often sheepish steps into the world of collecting. Since my move from collector to collector/dealer, I have been struck and indeed impressed by the number of "young" people who are enthusiastically venturing into our world and who, by their own to-be-commended brave admittance, don't know where or how to start. Perhaps this will make the process less overwhelming for them and they may enjoy the journey and the adventure of it all as much as I continue to do so.

The second half of the book will feature homes of existing and established 20th century collectors whose understanding of these basic principles of display have allowed them and their previously personal and private obsessions to boldly come out of the closet and proudly present themselves and their objects of passion to the delight, appreciation and admiration of us all.

A R T D E C

SCAPES

HOW TO USE THIS BOOK

OKAY, ALLOW me firstly to state how *not* to use this book. This book should not be used as some rigid, dully didactic carved in stone constitution, but rather employed and enjoyed as an idea starter for displaying of items from your own 20th Century collection, be it large or small. For let's face it, if you were to put any five designers in a room and have them take turns in grouping the same collection of items, not only would you likely receive a whole new appreciation of the merits of humility, but also five totally different solutions to the task at hand. There is *no* one way, there are *no* wrongs, but there are a lot of tricks to help you get it right and the purpose of this book is to let you in on some of them.

As a collector, I have always loved pairs of objects, and by pairs I not only mean two objects that have been designed to be placed with one another (i.e. book ended) but also two examples of exactly the same object. However, the interesting fact is that, in the display world, the visual strength of the pair is dramatically increased when a third or even contrasting object is added to the mix. In fact, in the world of inanimate objects, unlike its human relationship counterpart, the ménage à trois always works better.

And now, perhaps the most important and deservedly respected maxim — When creating a grouping, the magic number for some unknown reason, is seven. Most of us are familiar with The Magnificent Seven, The Group of Seven, The Seven Samurai, Seven Brides for Seven Brothers, The Seven Dwarfs, The G7, and The Seven Pillars of Wisdom. (And most of us know that some of the above met with more success than others.) However, I am here, dear readers, to let you into the triumph of the *Art Decoscapes* Seven, and should you apply it and learn to love it, then you will always be met with display success. Try it for yourself tonight at the dinner table. Indulge me. Just take any seven items from the table and arrange them in a group. Play with their color, size, alignment, similarities, or differences, and see for yourself how they will successfully lock together as a group (not withstanding the fact that your family will probably think that you have added obsessive compulsive disorder to your already chronic antique addiction, or worse that you have begun a regression into childhood and that the next step will be playing with your food).

After a short period of time (the precise length of which will probably be determined by the patience of your immediate family rather than by your achieved expertise), you will be able to graduate from objects on the dinner table to objects from your own collection. This is where this book comes in, and in its first section it will show you some of the many different ways that ingredients from your own collection can be grouped and displayed to their maximum advantage. It will demonstrate how the height and mass of different articles can work together. Watch how the color and tone of your items can be used to complement one another. Note how the items can be grouped by the materials that they are made of, by the manufacturer who produced them, by the subject matter, or by the fact that the items shared the same original function. Indeed, there are hundreds of ways that items can be grouped to bring an overall logic to their display. One of the most sobering lessons to a collector is that in order to create a display using just seven pieces, is that it is not necessary for those seven items have cost a lot of money. Just think back to the exercise at the dinner table, if it is not too painful a memory. The basic concept is that the successful grouping of a selection of objects from your collection will add a substantially increased visual value to each of the individual components.

As you meander through the examples in the theory section of *Art Decoscapes,* see how the size, weighting, and positioning of the items work together to form a cohesive whole. Then think of items from your own collection and how these concepts of display can be applied to them.

Earlier I stressed the successes of the *Art Decoscapes* Seven but the diligent reader will notice that the theory section also includes groupings with three, five, nine, and even eleven items that work very well. But that observant reader will also remember that I mentioned that there are no rules. To further prove that point, you will also find examples where eight items are grouped, but before you cry, "Hey, no fair, just wait a minute, you said only odd numbers work", you will see that on those occasions, two of the objects are visually grouped together as one unit. It really is true. Check it out for yourself. (You can believe me; after all I was in advertising.)

Having decided on the number of items from your 20th Century collection that you wish to display, it is now time for us to delve into antiquity in order to discover the key to composing these items. In order to master this, one could spend hours, weeks, and months studying countless scholarly tomes on the theory of the art of composition and in the end still be none the wiser.

As a result, I am going to try to simplify it, by distilling all that information and introducing you to the yet to be acknowledged elegant cleverness of the Chrome Triangle Theory. (The ancient world referred to this as the theory of the golden triangle probably because chrome had not been invented.) So here goes. If one opens almost any art work and looks at the successful paintings, photographs, or architecture, one can see that success has a unifying factor. The composition is based in some way or another on a triangle. Art history teaches us methods to discover the exact proportions of this golden triangle. But here's where the chrome triangle theory breaks away from academic thought. If one studies the groupings in the theory part of this book, and the accompanying schematic diagrams, one sees that the Chrome Triangle can be of many different proportions and can in fact be used in an endless variety of ways in a myriad of proportions. It can be right side up, on its side, or even upside down, as long as the arrangement of the items follows the basic shape of a triangle. You will soon find, as you arrange your own art decoscapes, that this compositional formula (for they are not rules but heartfelt and oft successfully proven suggestions) will become second nature and almost wonderfully subconscious.

I leave you with the words of Thomas A. Edison once quoted as having said, "Hell, there are no rules here; we are just trying to accomplish something." That "something" I may add, is a great deal of fun.

ART DEC

SCAPES

THE THEORY

THESE PINK LUCITE and black Bakelite items have been arranged in two equally effective ways. The picture on the right shows a symmetrical grouping with the bud vases and biscuit box anchoring the arrangement, whilst the cigarette

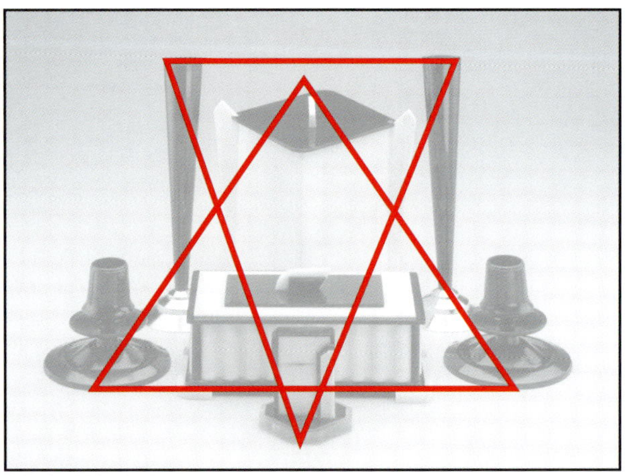

box and table lighter firmly centre the group, and two black candleholders provide bounding elements. On the following page is an asymmetrical arrangement of the same group of

objects in which the vases and biscuit box remain in the rear, with the vases balanced by the candleholders on the right and the biscuit box in turn balanced by the cigarette box on the left. The table lighter is purposely left open to add a seemingly random diagonal accent to this grouping. These two photographs simply serve to illustrate the point that there is more than one way to acheive a successfull arrangement of an identical group of items.

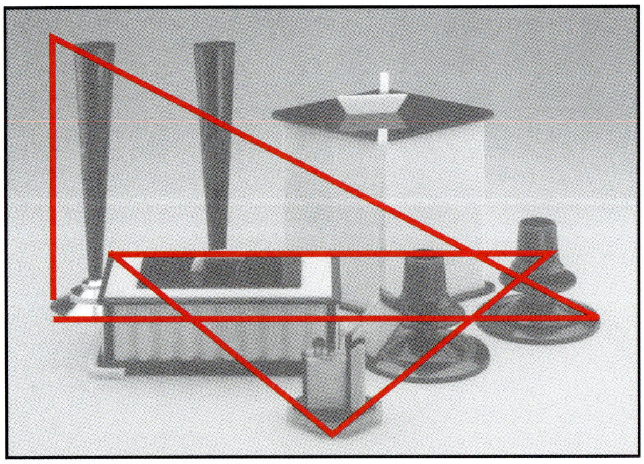

Clockwise from left: pair of American Bakelite and chrome bud vases attributed to Helen Dryden for The Dura Company, c.1936, $230-250. English Lucite and Bakelite unmarked biscuit box, c.1946, $225-250. English Lucite and Bakelite unmarked cigarette box and table lighter, c.1935, $250-275. English black Bakelite candleholders by Linder, c.1939, $125-150.

MANUFACTURERS and designers were quick to jump onto the "Saturn Bandwagon" that was created by the imagery in the logo of the 1933 Century of Progress Exhibition held in Chicago. No sooner did this planet imagery appear, than it started a design craze that permeated through a plethora of objects across the world and lasted well into the 50's. This arrangement features just some of these objects.

From left: Swedish Gense silver plated planet candlesticks, c.1955, $1650-1850. Pair of Canadian unmarked aluminum saturn lamps with gimped fiberglass canoe shades, c.1939, $750-850. Canadian Electrolier chrome and black enamel saturn lamp, c.1935, $650-850. American SOH Rochester chrome and enamel saturn lamp with star pierced shade, c.1935, $475-575. American Revere saturn ashtray in brass, chrome and Bakelite, c.1937, $150-175. American, unmarked anodized aluminum saturn ashtray, c.1940, $130-150.

BUTTERSCOTCH phenolic resins combine with pastel pink Lucite and just a hint of chrome in this seven piece arrangement from the United Kingdom. The group is held together by the large table clock in the centre while the pair of two-tone phenolic and pink Lucite candleholders are stepped to give an added dimension and depth.

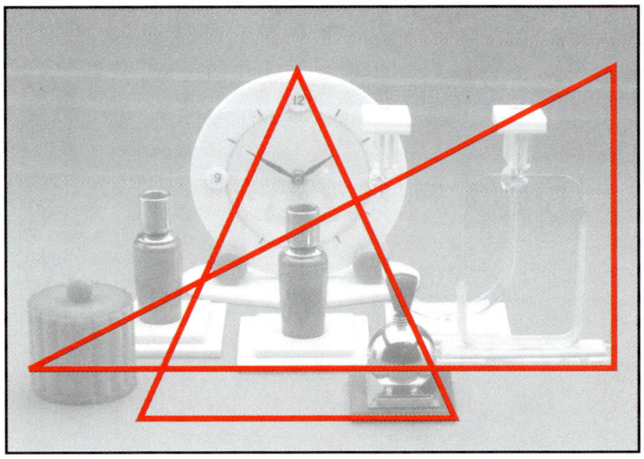

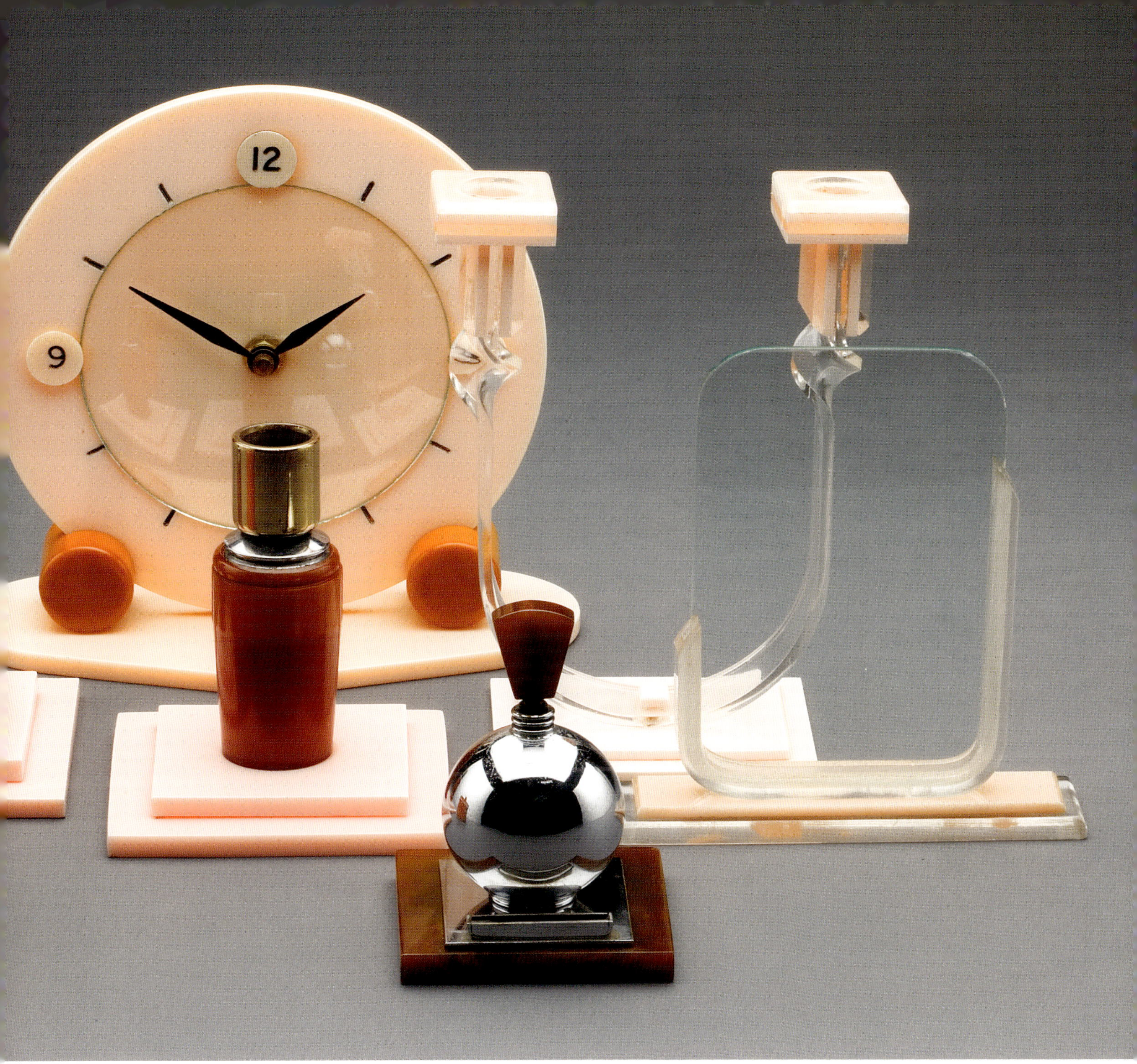

Clockwise from left: English, unmarked phenolic resin box, c.1930, $275-375. Pair of English unmarked two-tone phenolic resin and Lucite candleholders , c.1935, $275-325. Scottish phenolic resin and Lucite by Glen electric table clock, c.1939, $325-350. English unmarked 'U' based three color twin candleholder, c.1946, $125-150. English unmarked Lucite and glass photo frame, c.1946, $150-175. English unmarked Bakelite and chrome ball shaped table striker lighter, c.1935, $225-250.

WHEN PEOPLE think of Art Deco design they usually think of the cool look of chrome, but many of the manufacturers of the period also produced the same items in other finishes. The use of copper in this grouping gives a real warmth, whilst still maintaining that all-important Art Deco feel.

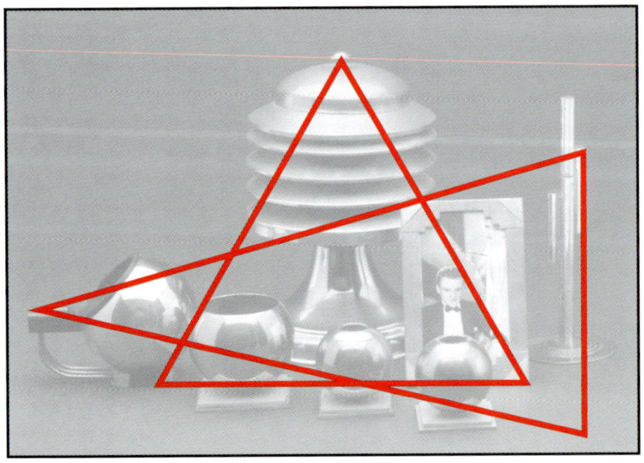

Clockwise from left; Belgian unmarked ball ashtray, c.1935, $175-225. Canadian 5 tiered Coulter lamp, c.1935, $425-475. American unmarked copper postcard frame, c.1929, $95-110. American Chase bud vase, c.1933, $125-150. American Chase Bubble candleholders and Bubble Flower Holder, c.1936, $325-350.

BLACK AND red teamed with chrome, probably the most typical colors of Art Deco, come together in this tall and highly geometric grouping. The English chrome lamp with its truly eccentric Lucite shade towers over the iconic style of the Mariani clock

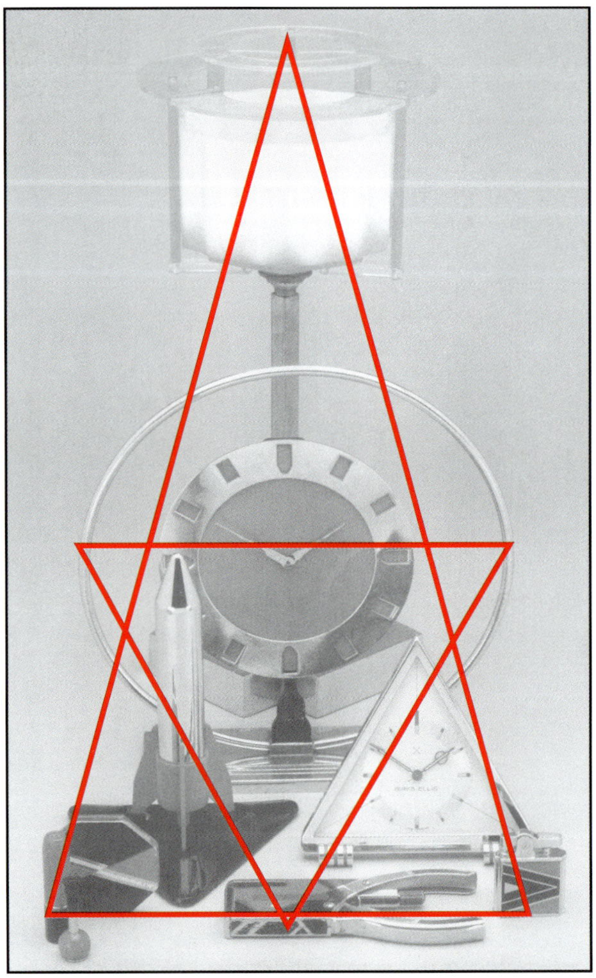

Clockwise from left; Canadian unmarked Bakelite cigarette holder, c.1939, $90-110. Japanese Weston lipstick lighter, c.1940, $50-75. Japanese unmarked hexagonal compact, c.1935, $200-235. Japanese unmarked Rocket table lighter, c.1955, $175-200. American Diecasters of New York mechanical clock by Mariani, c.1939, $1200-1500. English chrome lamp with tri-color Lucite shade c.1939, $1150-1250. German triangular desk clock retailed by Birks Ellis, c.1935, $375-425. Japanese Fisher wheel and flint lighter,. c.1947, $100-115. American geometric Red Star hand stapler, c.1935, $675-775.

BIRKS-ELLIS

SPHERES OF chrome proliferate in this elongated display, which would work equally well on a shelf, mantle piece or console table. The three German sphere clocks set the tone for this grouping and the theme is carried through in the two table lighters, the bosses for the pair of three arm candleholders, and even on the small chrome spheres that serve to hold the mirrored glass in place on the bases of the two free-standing photo frames on either side of the group.

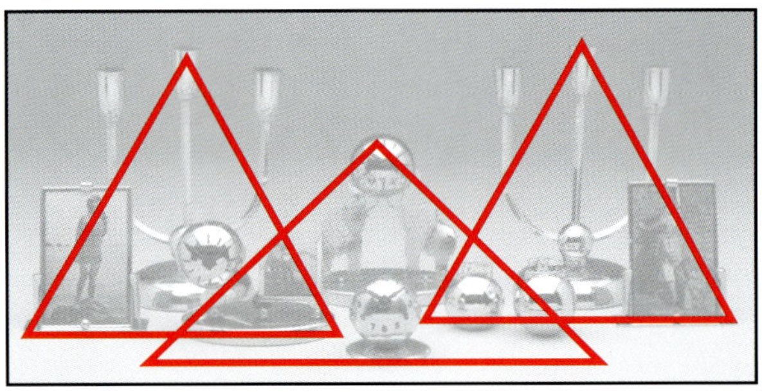

Clockwise from left; pair of English unmarked chrome postcard frames, c.1930, $285-300. Pair of German unmarked chrome triple candleholders, C.1930, $275-300. German unmarked chrome figural elephant ball clock, c.1930, $450-550. Japanese unmarked chrome ball table lighter, c.1935, $100-125. English chrome Orb table lighter, c.1935, $115-125. German unmarked chrome and black enamel ball clock, c.19-30, $375-450. German unmarked chrome ball desk clock with photo-frame c.1930, $550-650

CREAM CAN make a strong period statement no matter in what material it makes an appearance. In this grouping the cream appears in glass, enamel, Bakelite, Plaskon, plastic, and Catalyn, and all to great affect. The chrome and mirror accents effectively heighten the Art Deco period feel in a very graphic way.

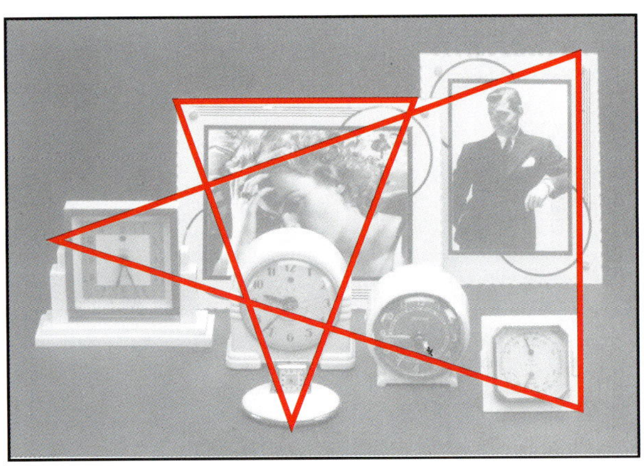

Clockwise from left; English Temco Bakelite electric desk clock, c.1945, $175-225. American unmarked reverse painted landscape photo-frame, c.1940, $225-250. American unmarked reverse painted portrait photo-frame, c.1940, $225-250. American Taylor Hemiguide barometer, c.1935, $50-75. American Ingraham Catalin electric clock, c.1939, $150-175. American Warren Telechron Plaskon alarm clock, c.1938, $140-170. German unmarked enamel and chrome watch-compact, c.1930, $350-450.

Clockwise from left; German ceramic Ronson butane lighter, c.1960, $90-100. American Medco cocktail shakers, c.1940, $75-100 each. French unmarked plaster bust, c.1930, $275-300. American Ingraham purse watch, c.1940, $175-200. English unmarked ceramic pipe rest, c.1935, $75-100. American Filto pipe, c.1946, $75-100. English Barklay wheel and flint table lighter, c.1935, $150-200. American Reich-Ash powder box, c.1935, $100-125.

THE BRIGHT REDS in this grouping are contrasted by the rich tones of cream and chrome. The three Medco cocktail shakers are placed on the diagonal and set the style for this unconventional but very effective arrangement.

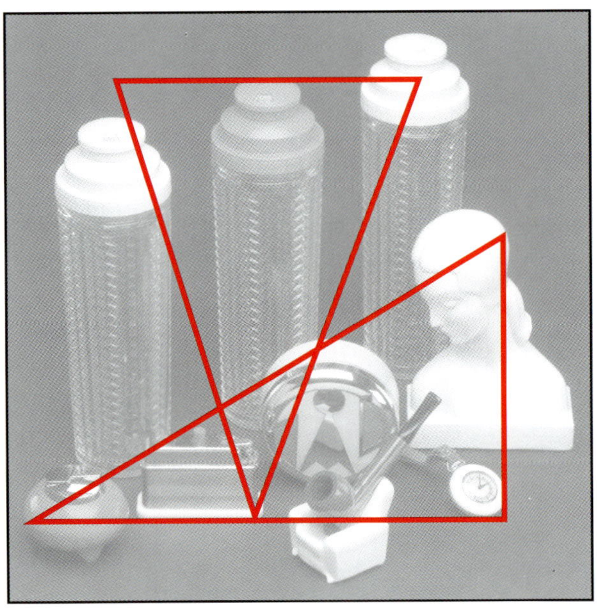

BURL BLONDE WOOD accented with ebony or rosewood is a combination that one often finds in the stylish European cocktail bars and furniture of the Art Deco period. The wonderfully designed English clock in the centre of this group is actually a craftsman made piece. All the items in this grouping originate in either England or France.

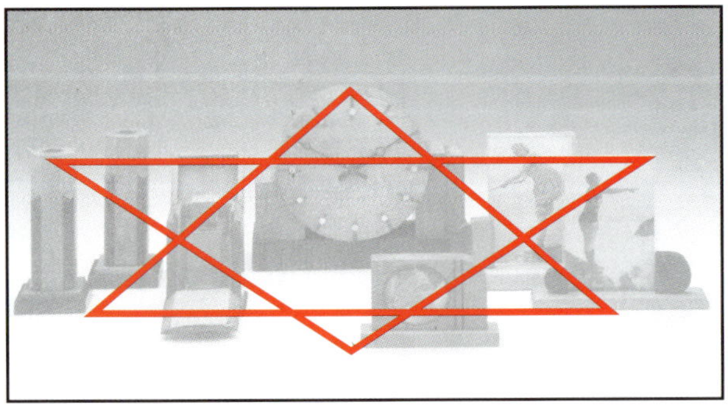

Clockwise from left; pair of English unmarked pillar cadlesticks, c.1930, $125-150. French unmarked boxed perfume bottle, c.1929, $300-350. English unmarked craftsmen made veneer and mother-of-pearl Garrard movement mantle clock, c.1935, $1500-1750. Pair of French unmarked postcard frames, c.1930, $195-225. American unmarked machine age wood frame, c.1942, $100-125.

A SINGLE SPLASH OF red on the base of the tall trumpet vase brings added interest to this grouping featuring a black circle motif. The Bakelite handles and ingeniously designed sugar and creamer that nest as a single circle work to echo the tubular black supports of the English mantle clock.

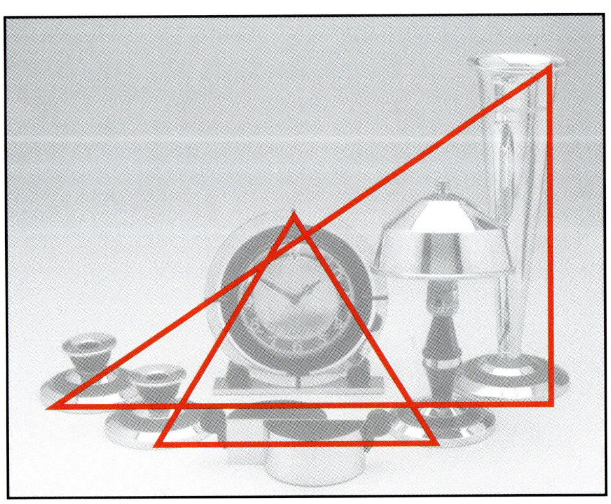

Clockwise from left; pair of American S.O.H. Rochester candlesticks, c.1935, $125-175. French Metamec mechanical mantle clock, c.1939, $350-425. American S.O.H. Rochester trumpet vase, c.1935, $200-225. American S.O.H. Rochester accent lamp, c.1935, $225-275. American unmarked nesting cream and sugar, c.1938, $150-200.

LUCITE WAS invented in the 30's but its use exploded during the 40's and 50's. The marvellous color combinations on the two Canadian clocks are truly outstanding. The brazen pose of the standing nude silhouette from the 50's contrasts nicely with the somewhat demure look of the pair of 30's sitting nudes. Lucite picture frames can be found in a variety of styles, and to me always conjure up visions of the imagined film star boudoirs of Hollywood in the 40's.

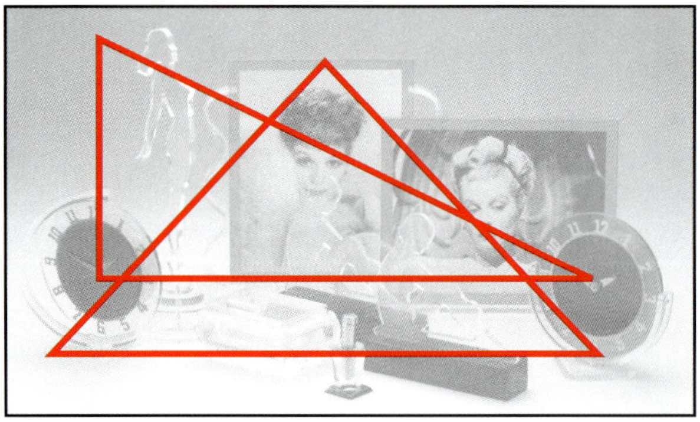

Clockwise from left; Canadian unmarked tri-color Lucite mechanical clock, c.1946, $200-250. American unmarked Lucite nude, c.1939, $150-175. American unmarked Lucite photo-frame, c.1946, $175-200. English unmarked Lucite photo-frame, c.1946, $150-175. Canadian unmarked tri-color Lucite mechanical clock, c.1946, $200-250. Pair of unmarked English Lucite and wood figural bookends, c.1939, $225-250. Canadian unmarked Lucite wheel and flint table lighter, c.1939, $40-60. Canadian unmarked Lucite cigarette box, c.1939, $100-150.

CHROME AND BLACK shiny Bakelite combine to make a strong visual statement. The ingeniously designed English Bakelite domino set is complemented nicely by the pair of plastic saddle shoes. The clean lines of the black Bakelite and chrome Jumbo table lighter lock together with its Penguin lighter counterpart. The display is held together by the electric Mariani table clock.

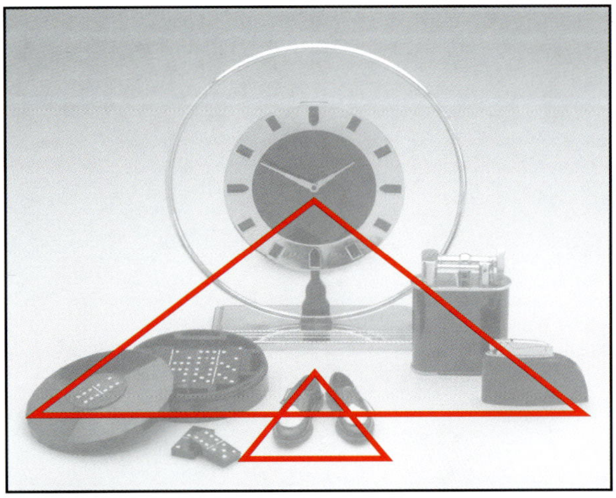

Clockwise from left; English Molde Products Ltd. pocket domino set, c.1935, $250-275. American Die Casters of New York electric table clock by Mariani, c.1939, $1200-1500. English Jumbo lift arm table lighter, c.1935, $200-250. Japanese penguin wheel and flint table lighter, c.1939, $100-125. Hong Kong unmarked plastic miniature saddle shoes, c.1950, $50-75.

BLACK BAKELITE accented with chrome enhances the round shapes of the Dura elephant bridge marker, the cue ball lighter, plus the very graphic English clock, and contrast very effectively with the linear stepped design of both the picture frame and the Walter Dorwin Teague designed Stormguide barometer.

Clockwise from left; American Taylor Stormguide barometer, c.1935, $200-250. English unmarked mechanical table clock, c.1930, $250-300. American unmarked Bakelite and chrome table frame, c.1935, $225-275. American La Parfaite by NTS, Bakelite vanity powder box, c.1930, $125-150. American Bentley wheel and flint table lighter, c.1946, $100-125. American Dura figural elephant bridge marker, c.1935, $100-125. American Q-Ball wheel and flint table lighter, c.1940, $100-125.

B ROWN BAKELITE in the era between the wars was seen everywhere, in items that ranged from the utilitarian to the really excitingly designed art objects. Here the splendidly executed machine age design of the American Penwood Telechron electrical clock is flanked by two classic English Lindsden Ware candleholders. The rounded lines of the desk lamp blend nicely with the pair of French Parure vases whose shape is echoed by the English Gillette razor box in the foreground.

Clockwise from left; pair of French unmarked Parure de Pendule vases, c.1935, $175-200. Pair of English Lindsden Ware candlesticks, c.1939, $400-600. Czechoslovakian unmarked adjustable desk lamp, c.1946, $500-575. American Penwood Telechron electric digital clock, c.1950, $550-600. English Gillette razor and box, c.1946, $75-100

SYMMETRY AND CIRCULAR motifs are the keynotes of this grouping, and the American lighter in the foreground displays both. It leads one's eye onto the small round Japanese Toyo clock and the English steel mantle clock. The grouping is bounded by the Commodore ashtray and cigarette holder set by Danbury, and by the pair of Mid-Century designed candleholders.

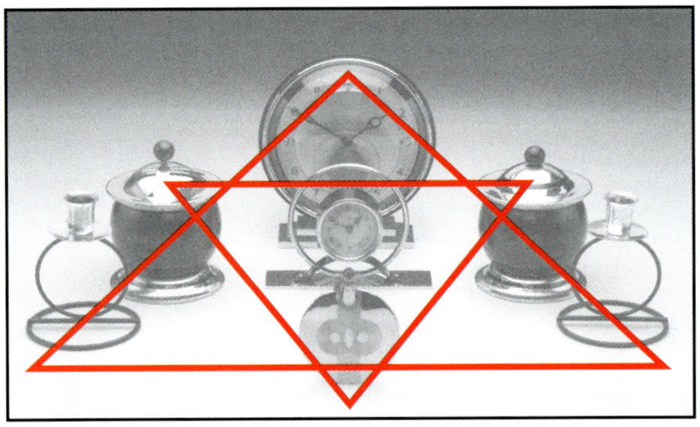

Clockwise from left; pair of unmarked American candlesticks, c.1960, $100-125. American Danbury Commodore ashtray and humidor set, c.1935, $225-250. English Temco electric mantle clock, c.1940, $250-300. American unmarked geometric wheel and flint lighter, c.1938, $200-250. Japanese Toyo desk clock, c.1939, $175-250.

GENTS' ACCESSORIES

are here grouped in a wonderful combination of burgundy and cream and in a variety of materials. Whilst the small English shaving brush on the left is genuine ivory, the one on the right is in French Ivory. The three HIS bottles have Bakelite heads and glass bodies, while the ziggurat lamp in the rear is unusual in that it is made completely of plastic.

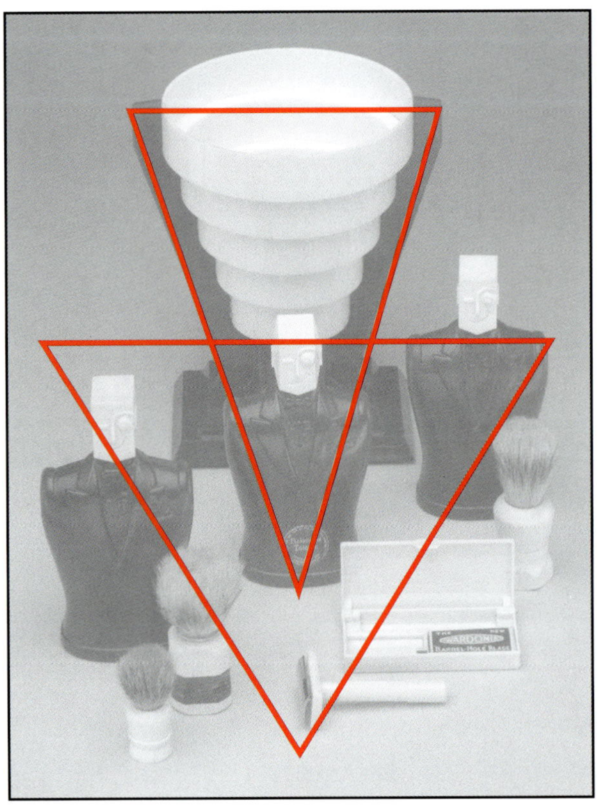

Clockwise from left; English unmarked ivory shaving brush, c.1960, $100-125. American unmarked enamel shaving brush, c.1950, $35-40. Pair of American HIS cologne bottles, by Glenn Claypoole for DeBeaujois, c.1946, $400-425 each. American HIS talc bottle with paper label, c.1946, $425-450. American unmarked French Ivory shaving brush, c.1940, $35-40. English Wardonia razor and box, c.1945, $100-125.

HIS
Balanced Talcum
WARDONIA
THE NEW
WARDONIA
BARREL-HOLE BLADE

METROPOLIS style imagery and industrial forms make up this grouping and are emphasized by the extreme design of the iconic Mar-Le frame in the rear. The two graphically excellent Kwikway fans book end the machine age group in the front. The 'V' shape of the fantastic bud vase in the centre provides a foil for the vertical lines featured in all the other items.

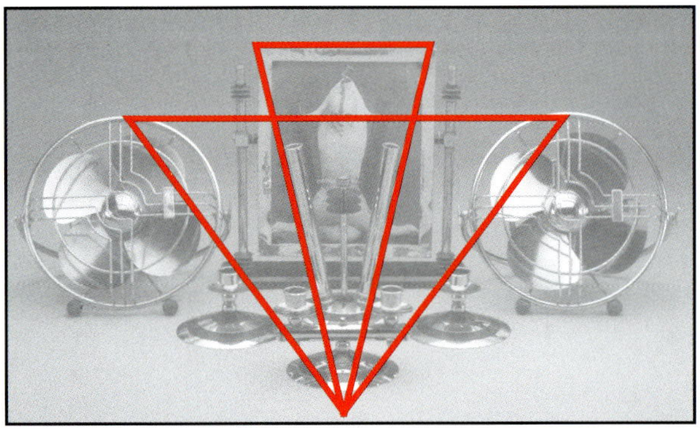

Clockwise from left; pair of American Kwik-Way desk fans, c.1942, $350-400. American Mar-Le aluminum and wood photo-frame, c.1935, $300-375. Pair of American unmarked candlesticks, c.1935, $200-250. American unmarked twin candleholder, c.1935, $250-300. American unmarked twin bud vase, c.1935, $275-325.

THIS GROUPING of wonderfully designed stepped chrome English FoFrames displays all seven sizes in which these ingeniously structured swing corner frames were produced. Placed in descending order by size, they make a very effective arrangement with the two smallest breaking rank in the foreground.

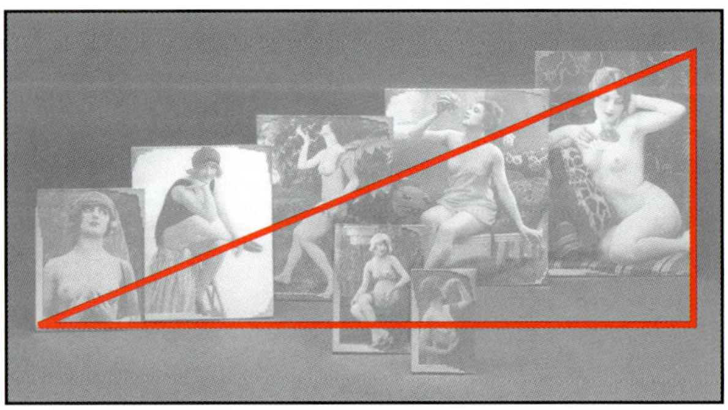

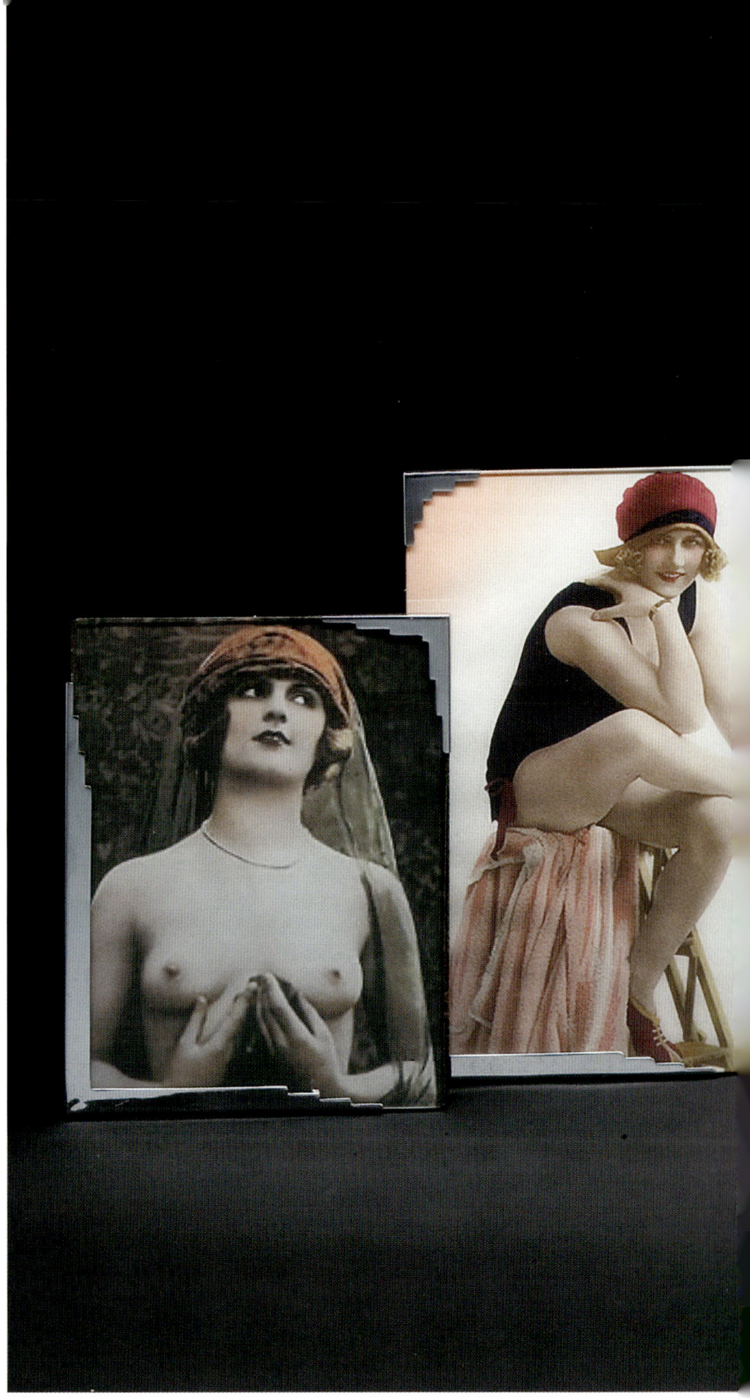

Clockwise from left; English chrome adjustable FoFrames, c.1930, size, 6"x8", $175, size, 8"x10", $200, size, 8"x11", $225, size, 10"x12", $275, size, 10"x14", $300, size, 3.5"x6", $125, and size, 5"x7", $150.

HOLLYWOOD TONES of aqua, green and eau de nil link this grouping of items, but all originated in England. The classic tennis ball ashtray tones in nicely with an ashtray that was originally designed for the RMS Queen Mary. The biomorphic shapes of the chrome candleholders from the 30's echo nicely the translucent flourishes on the arms of the Lucite frames from the 40's.

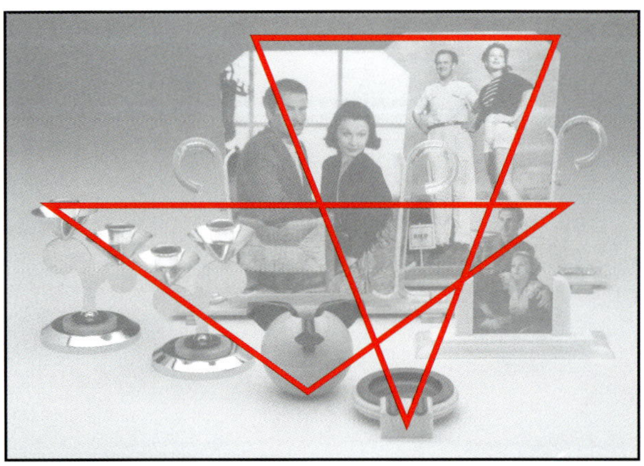

Clockwise from left; pair of unmarked English candleholders, c.1935, $275-325. Pair of English unmarked Lucite table frames, c.1946, $400-500. English Lucite postcard frame, c.1939, $125-150. English British Buttner cigarette ashtray, c.1937, $250-300. English Roanoid ball ash tray, c.1935, $400-450.

DIED

ALUMINUM appears here in a variety of objects, and combines to form this extremely powerful grouping. The vertical repeating circles of the candleholders in the background together with the glass ball on the torchiere provide an excellent foil for the horizontal circles on the machine age design of the postal scale, pipe and pipe lighter in the foreground.

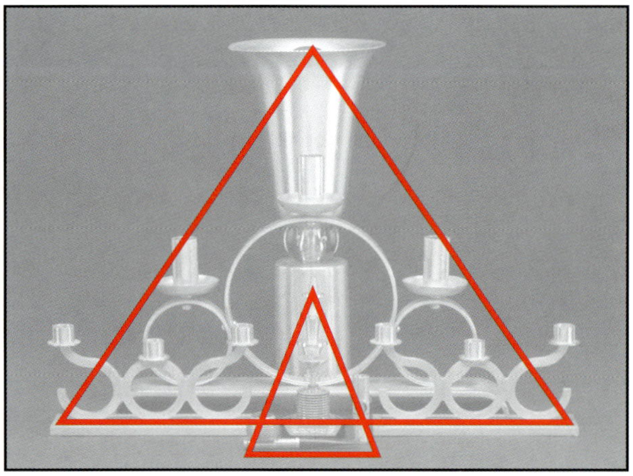

Clockwise from left; pair of American unmarked triple aluminum candleholders, c.1942, $200-275. American unmarked triple aluminum candleholder, c.1945, $400-425. American unmarked aluminum table torchiere, c.1942, $300-400. American Nimrod wheel and flint pipelighter, c.1945, $50-75. American Yellow Bowl aluminum pipe, c.1942, $125-150. American Thomson Engineering postal scale, c.1942, $115-135.

WOOD TONES AND chrome take their cue from the miniature mantle clock and set the mood for this grouping of French and English items. The diagonal lines created by the curved asymmetrical pillars of the picture frames and the arms of the triple candleholders lead our eye to the charming wood, chrome and Bakelite baby brush and cream jar in the centre of the composition.

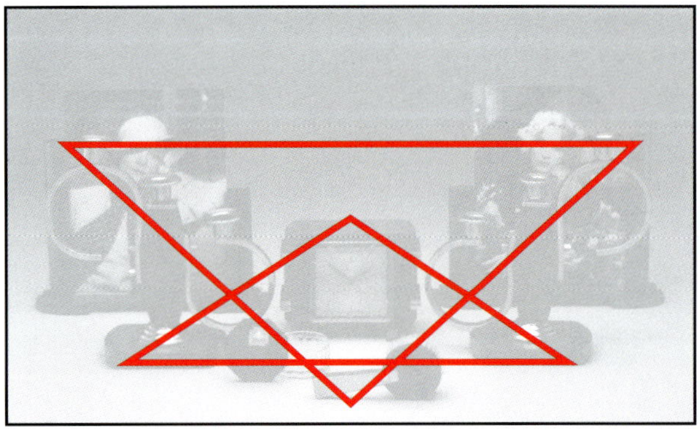

Clockwise from left; pair of English unmarked oak table frames, c.1939, $250-300. French Bayard mechanical mantle clock, c.1935, $400-450. Pair of Belgian unmarked triple candleholders, c.1935, $350-400. French unmarked baby brush and cream jar set, c.1930, $175-225.

SAD SARAH, THE BASHFUL Bride, and the Reluctant Virgin are all names that I have heard to describe the Cubist nudes that decorate this fascinating range of Farber items. There are many more products in the line, but this charming grouping demonstrates that it is not necessary to own every piece in a range to make an extremely effective and interesting display.

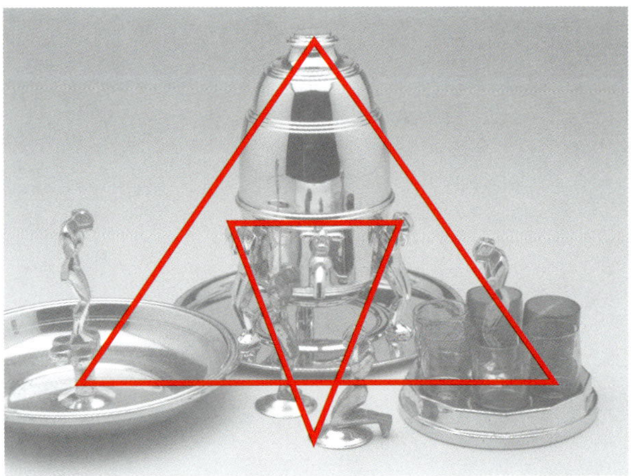

Clockwise from left; American Farber figural ashtray, c.1936, $240-275. American Farber figural liqueur dispenser with tray, c.1936, $275-325. American Farber figural liqueur glass tray, c.1936, $250-275. American Farber nude kneeling, c.1936, $45-55. American Farber nude standing, c.1936, $45-55.

A SONG FROM THE English musical hall, 'Leanin' On The Lamp post' was doubtless the inspiration for the candleholder that is the high point of the dark red and chrome grouping. Flanked on the right by the 50's ball ashtray and on the left by the table compact, this arrangement features three table lighters and a French musical alarm clock.

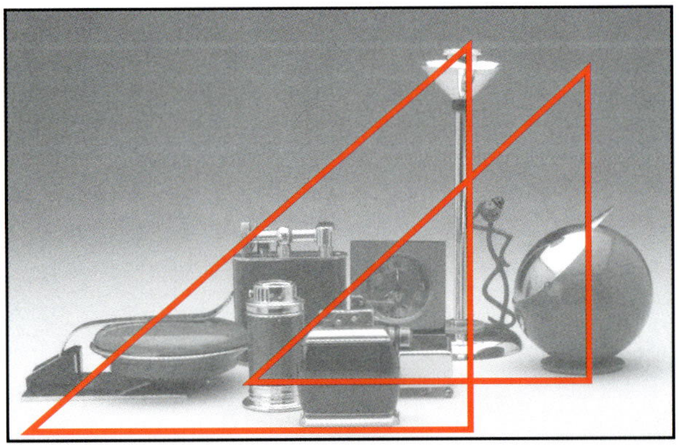

Clockwise from left; English unmarked chrome and Bakelite table compact, c.1935, $150-225. English leather wrapped Jumbo lift arm table lighter, c.1935, $225-250. French unmarked musical alarm clock, c.1939, $225-250. English unmarked chrome and Bakelite candleholder, c.1939, $175-200. German Quist ball ashtray, c.1958, $65-85. German chrome and Bakelite wheel and flint table lighter, c. 1940, $150-175. American Chase Automatic table lighter, c.1933, $100-125.

THE LARGE black glass round face of the Dutch clock nicely centres this geometric aluminum grouping. The rigid Machine Age design of the candleholders, frames, lighters, and pipe is relieved by the frivolity of the French cockatoo cocktail stick holder.

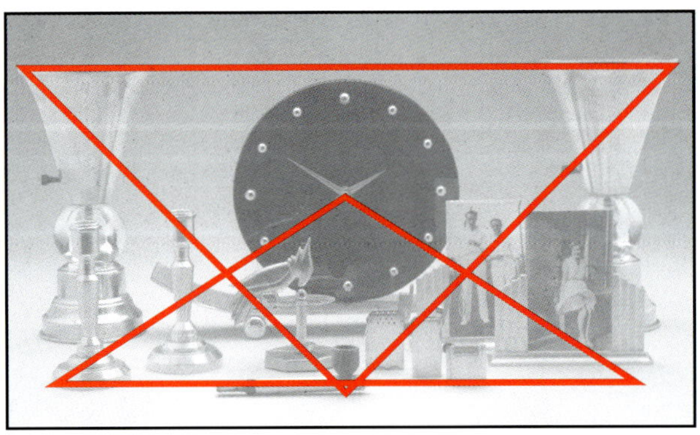

Clockwise from center: American unmarked footed aluminum and wood pipe, c.1942, $125-150. French unmarked figural cockatoo cocktail stick holder, c.1939, $125-150. Pair of American unmarked aluminum candleholders, c.1950, $150-175. Pair of American unmarked aluminum and glass table torchieres, c.1942, $250-350. Dutch unmarked aluminum and Vitrolite electric mantle clock, c.1939, $750-850. Pair of English unmarked aluminum postcard frames, c.1939, $275-300. American Cleveland wheel and flint pocket lighter, c.1942, $75-100. English Lord Oxford wheel and flint pocket lighter, c.1939, $75-100. English Buffalo Dub-L-ite wheel and flint pocket lighter, c.1939, $100-125.

THE COMBINATION OF ebony and ivory colors in this collection of chrome cigarette cases, compacts, and lighters is given height and mass by the matching colors of the cream glass banded shade on the chrome and black Markel desk lamp that serves to anchor the arrangement on the left.

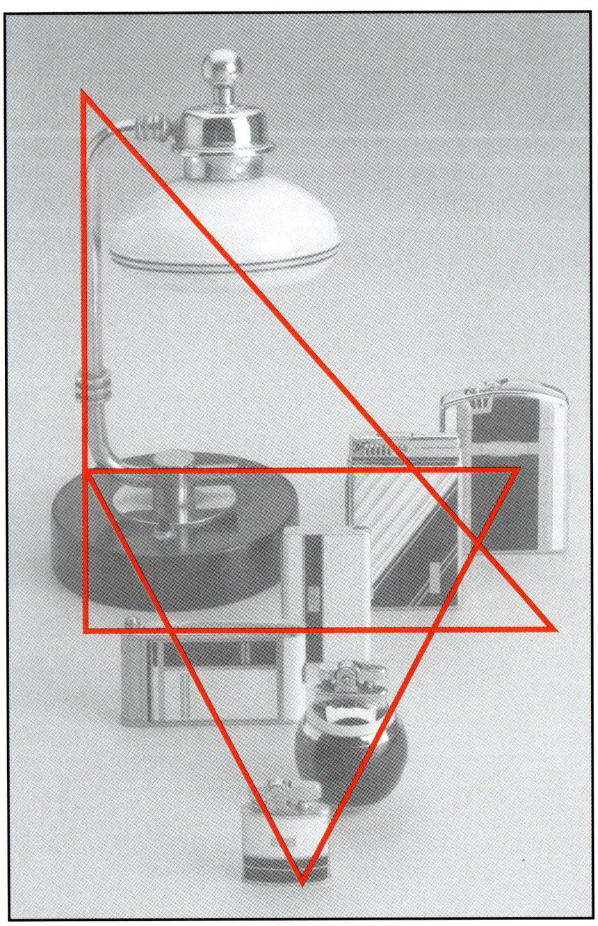

From front; Japanese Fisher wheel and flint pocket lighter, c.1942, $75-100. English Ronson Rondelite wheel and flint table lighter, c.1936. $150-250. German unmarked camera compact, c.1935, $200-250. American Bourjois compact, c.1940, $125-150. Japanese Hudson wheel and flint lighter/cigarette case combination, c.1940, $150-175. American Markel desk lamp, c.1932, $900-1000. American Ronson Twentycase wheel and flint lighter/cigarette case combination, c.1939, $200-250.

SHADES OF GREEN IN glass, anodized aluminum, Bakelite, enamelled plaster, pearlized paint and ceramic combine beautifully in this group. The elegant angled leg of the English plaster nude creates a wonderful right side angle to the grouping, while the geometric forms of the Canadian reverse-painted bar tray hold the group together.

Clockwise from left; American unmarked machine age accent lamp, c.1939, $300-400. English unmarked vase, c.1945, $150-200. Canadian unmarked reverse painted tray, c.1935, $375-425. English Leonardi plaster nude, c.1935, $350-400. American unmarked metal and ceramic box, c.1955, $250-300. English Smiths mechanical cradle clock, c.1939, $300-375. American Crystal Vue desk clock, c.1935, $300-350.

I N THE BAD OLD DAYS a coffee and a cigarette always went together, and in this grouping the tradition lives on. Here Harmony coffee services dating from the 30's and 40's and made by Manning-Bowman are displayed with a pair of "Gypsy" chrome and Bakelite ash-trays designed by Jay Ackerman.

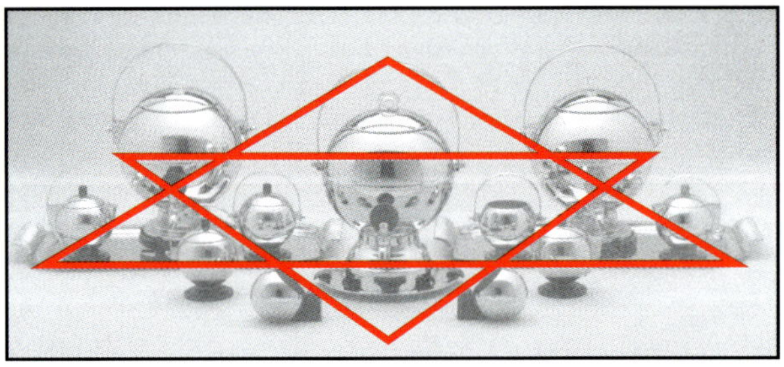

From front; pair of American Manning Bowman Gypsy ashtrays by Jay Ackerman, c.1941, $125-145. American Manning Bowman 940 four piece coffee service, c.1953, $350-400. American Manning Bowman Harmony chrome and black Bakelite four piece coffee service, c.1937, $375-475. American Manning Bowman Harmony chrome and Arlite four piece coffee service, c.1937, $400-500.

THE MODERN PLASTICS OF their time, Bakelite, Catalin, and Lucite, are featured here with ceramic and paint in this eclectic international arrangement. The only connection that these items share is their combined color scheme and this grouping uses this to its best advantage.

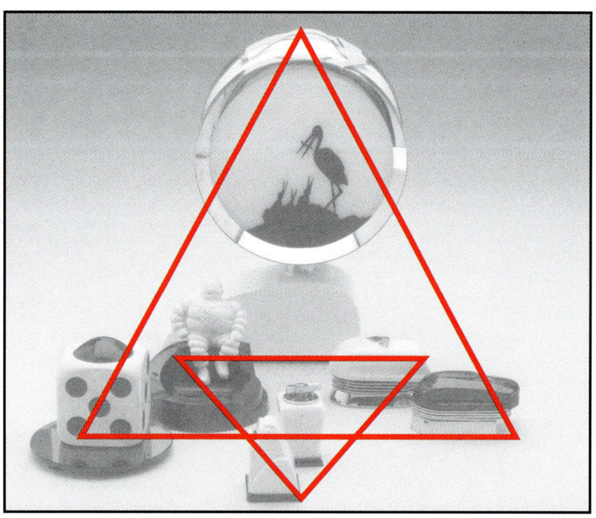

Clockwise from left; French Clic-Clac ceramic cigarette box, c.1939, $250-275. American Bibendum ashtray, c.1940, $225-250. English unmarked Bakelite and chrome child's night-light, c.1945, $475-550. Norwegian Ronning travelling iron, c.1945, $120-140. English Smoothie travelling iron, c.1939, $150-175. Japanese Fisher wheel and flint table lighter, c.1939, $80-100. American Listerine ceramic frog blade dispenser, c.1939, $75-100.

BRUSHED FINISHED METAL accented with polished metal and black give this group an air of sophisticated style. The severe skyscraper of the Canadian electric clock is softened by both the curved lines of the candleholders on the right, and the tiered American desk lamp.

From left; American unmarked 3 tiered desk lamp, c.1935, $300-350. American WIRA aluminum and Bakelite cigarette box, c.1940, $90-100. Canadian Sangamo skyscraper electric desk clock, c.1935, $325-350. Pair of Belgian silvered metal and ebonised wood triple candleholders, c.1935, $350-400.

DISCS AND SPHERES complement one another as these items from three decades are grouped together. Two frosted glass and chrome boudoir lamps flank two iconic designs from the world of American bar ware. The table lighter and spinner ash tray set from the 50's was probably inspired by the then current UFO craze.

Clockwise from left; pair of American unmarked boudoir lights, c.1935, $850-1000. American Spherical Miracle Thermos jug by Nowland and Schladermundt, c.1937, $175-275. American sods siphon by Bel Geddes and Paxton for The Walter Kidder Co., c.1938, $200-250. Japanese UFO wheel and flint table lighter and spinner ashtray set, c.1958, $100-125. American Chase Fireball table lighter, c.1936, $125-150.

THE ICE BLUE COLOR of the anodized and ribbed English Kaymet vase sets the tone for the matching his and hers Westclox bedside clocks that flank it. In front, the light blue glass of the English mantle clock is echoed by the blue glass in the cigarette dispenser, the cocktail cups, and the ingeniously constructed ashtray.

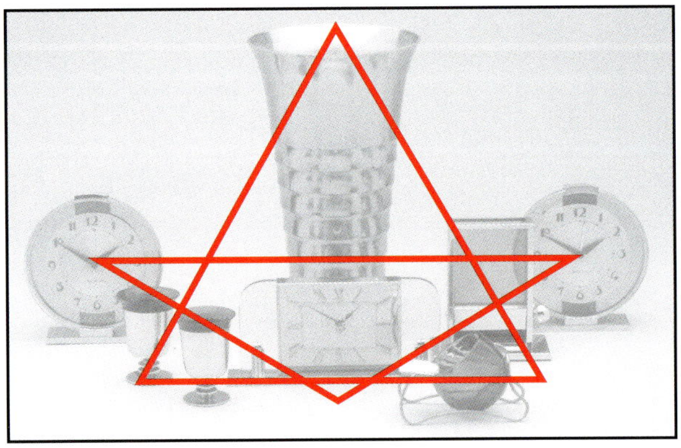

Clockwise from left; pair of Canadian Westclox electric bedside clocks, c.1939, $250-275 each. English Kaymet anodized aluminum vase, c.1945, $300-350. German chrome and glass cigarette dispenser, c.1939, $250-300. American Sandquist ashtray, c.1938, $175-200. English Smiths mechanical desk clock, c.1939, $275-325. Pair of unmarked American chrome and glass cocktail cups attributed to Walter Von Nessen, c.1935, $50-75 each.

THE TRADITIONAL BLUE of Art Deco is shown here in its deep cobalt glory. The anodized English Kaymet bowl acts as a backdrop for the complementary hued American cheese dish. The rich cobalt blues of the Chase pieces match the glass accents of the German clock, and tone in well with the blue and chrome of the table lighter in front.

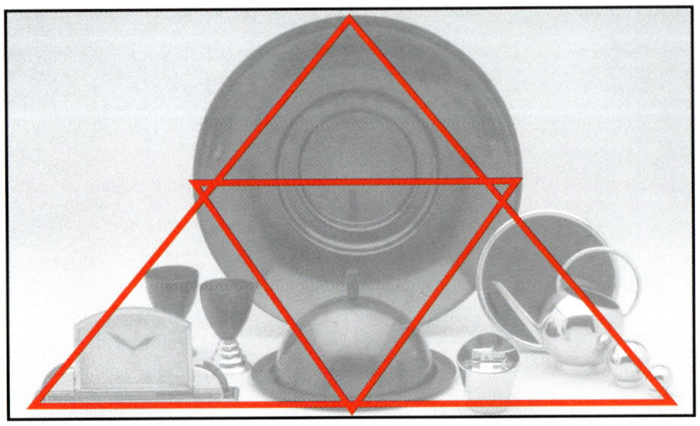

Clockwise from left; German chrome and blue glass mechanical desk clock, c.1935, $300-375. Pair of Chase Blue Moon cocktail cups, c.1936, $50-75 each. English Kaymet anodized aluminum fruit bowl, c.1945, $225-250. American Chase four piece Pancake and Corn set by Russel Wright, c.1935, $450-550. German Ronson butane wheel and flint table lighter, c.1965, $65-85. American unmarked anodized aluminum cheese dish, c.1955, $75-100.

Brown Bakelite is here brightened up with a hand painted polychrome parchment shade. The RCA tear drop record player is balanced with a diagonal row of four American clocks and a barometer, in styles that range from Art Deco to Machine Age. The two organic English Bakelite frames with tinted photographs add color on the right.

Clockwise from left; American Telechron electric digital clock, c.1940, $200-275.English unmarked lamp with hand painted shade, c.1945, $750-850.Canadian RCA CJM3 teardrop phonograph, c.1939, $400-450. Pair of English unmarked postcard frames, c.1939, $175-225. French Calor electric table lighter, c.1930, $250-300. American Hammond Junior electric clock, c.1938, $175-225. American Fee and Stemwedel Airguide barometer, c.1939. $125-150. American geometric electric clock, c.1930, $200-275.

DANCING PLASTER LADIES in ivory pearlescent painted dresses swirl around an English Temco Bakelite electric bedside clock in this charming and eclectic vanity group. They are flanked by an English Beswick honey glazed jug, while a French three piece solid ivory geometric brush and mirror set is placed on the diagonal and centered to lead the eye into the composition.

Clockwise from left; American unmarked dancing plaster figure, c.1940, $175-200. American unmarked dancing plaster figure, c.1940, $175-200. English Beswick matte glaze jug by Owen, c.1936, $100-125. French unmarked solid ivory vanity mirror and brushes, c.1929, $1500-2000. English Temco Bakelite electric desk clock, c.1945, $175-225.

TEMCO

ORANGE AND red provide a splash of color in this all chrome group, as an English table centre fruit bowl is flanked by its matching candleholders. The pair of tall Thermos flasks provide height to this arrangement whilst a pair of English FoFrames and a pair of organic French miniature frames thread through the arrangement.

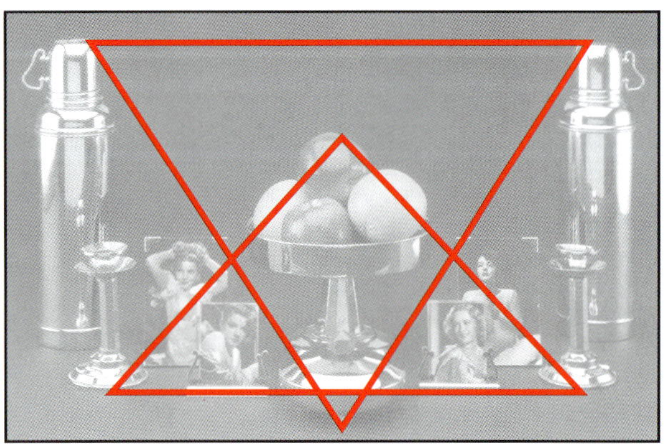

From left; pair of French Thermid Stable flasks, c.1945, $125-150. Pair of English unmarked stepped candlesticks, c.1935, $175-200. Pair of English FoFrame postcard frames, c.1935, $250-275. Pair of French unmarked chrome photo-frames, c.1930, $175-225. English unmarked chrome powder bowl, c.1935, $135-165. English unmarked chrome fruit bowl, c.1935, $175-225.

THIS FIGURAL ENGLISH companion set acts as a really interesting and strong centre point for this grouping. Its basic mass is echoed by the strongly designed and architectural English chrome mantle clock on the left, and the English chrome swivel frame on the right. The quirkily designed German ashtray clock is flanked by three equally eccentric ally designed lighters

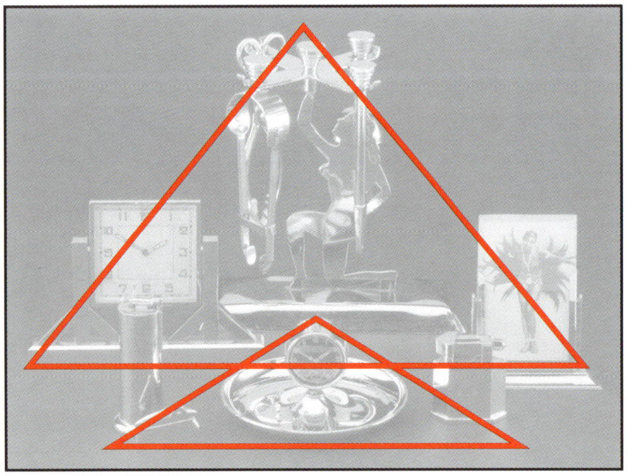

Clockwise from left; English unmarked architectural chrome mechanical mantle clock, c.1939, $325-375. English unmarked figural companion set, c.1935, $500-600. English unmarked postcard frame, c.1930, $175-200. English Talent lift arm table lighter, c.1930, $225-250. German unmarked mechanical clock/ashtray, c.1935, $250-275. Japanese Harvester Dove wheel and flint lighter, c.1950, $55-75. English Parker lift arm column table lighter, c.1935, $175-200.

NICKEL TONES FROM just one item bring a warmth to this otherwise all chrome arrangement. The massive Revere water pitcher stands firmly behind a Canadian jet engine cocktail shaker, while the film star in the French chrome picture frame has her eyes firmly fixed on the large English station master's watch.

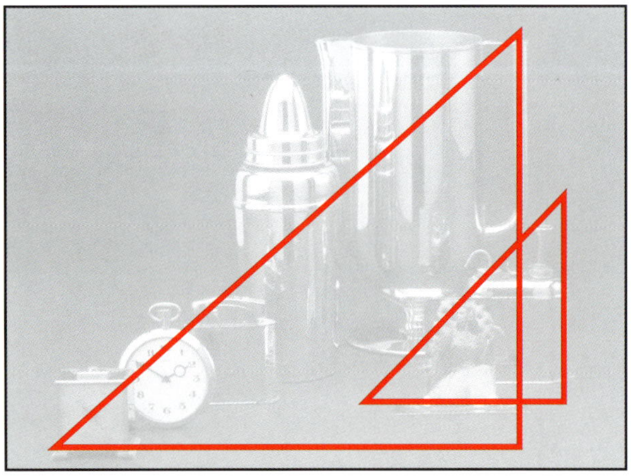

Clockwise from left; German unmarked mechanical alarm clock, c.1935, $100-125. English Smiths large pocket watch, c.1958, $125-160. French Myon wheel and flint table lighter, c.1939, $125-175. Canadian Babcock cocktail shaker, c.1945, $300-375. American Revere Baron water pitcher, c.1935, $200-275. American Thorens lighter fuel dispenser, c.1940, $275-300. French unmarked chrome photo-frame, c.1935, $100-125.

A GROUP of just some of the myriad of chrome photo frames produced in France between the wars. Their varied shapes and overall design look great when placed all together, whether they hold either period or contemporary photographs.

These French unmarked photo and postcard frames all date from the late 1930's and range in price from $75-325 each.

HERE THE ENGLISH candleholders, the French picture frames, and even the cigarettes in the German table cigarette holder, are all mirror images of each other. The dome shade of the lamp is echoed both by the ring handle of the cigarette holder and the sphere shape of the globe table lighter. The cigarettes are further locked in by the incised bands on the lamp.

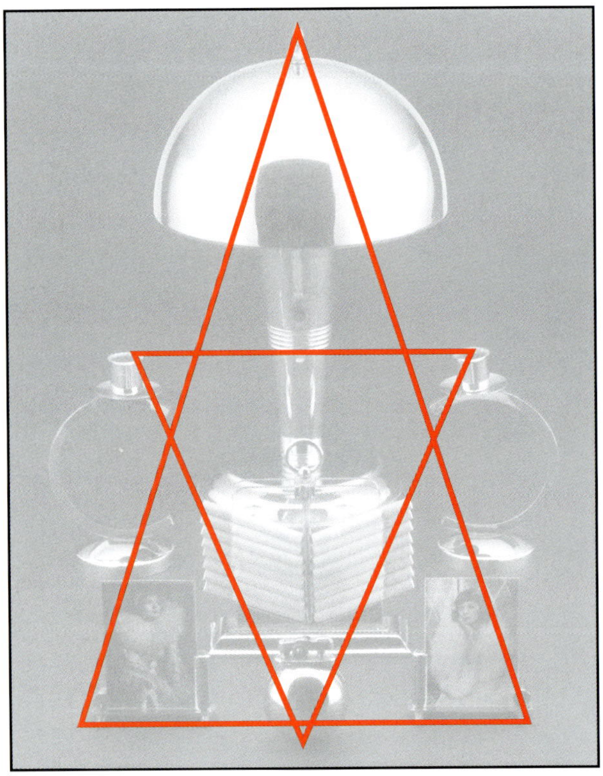

From front; Austrian Auer wheel and flint ball table lighter, c.1940, $100-150. Pair of French unmarked geometric photo-frames, c.1930, $200-250. German unmarked chrome and glass cigarette dispenser, c.1939, $250-275. Pair of unmarked English chrome candlesticks, c.1935, $200-250. American unmarked dome shaded accent lamp, c.1939, $450-550.

A CLEVERLY designed French adjustable ball table lamp from the 60's is mirrored by the American globe Plexiglas phone on the left, and by a Canadian ball ashtray on the right. The four spherical Chase pieces sit well with the pair of chrome spherical ring boxes in the center and front.

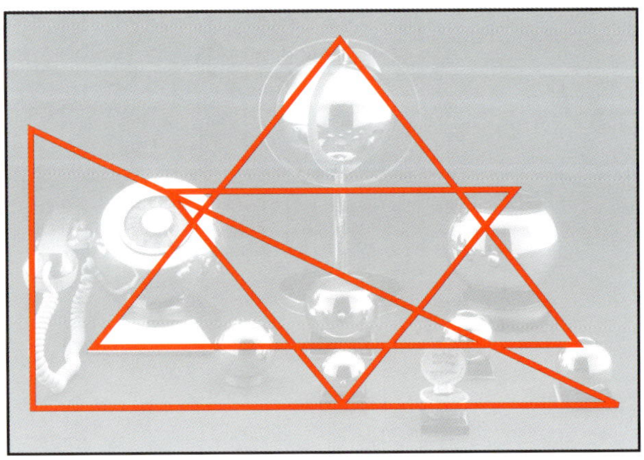

Clockwise from left; American unmarked chrome and Plexi ball phone, c.1968, $350-375. French unmarked adjustable shade desk lamp, c.1950, $550-650. Canadian unmarked chrome and enamel ball ashtray, c.1960, $100-150. American Chase bubble candlesticks and bubble flower holder, c.1935, $275-325. Pair of American Bluebird bubble ring boxes, c.1935, $200-225. American Chase Sugar Sphere, c.1937, $75-100.

A GROUP OF green accented items from various decades, with the shape of the bizarrely designed desk lamp in the background repeated by the Asprey shagreen and chrome match holder in the foreground. A Kaymet vase on the left is balanced by a pair of yacht bookends on the right.

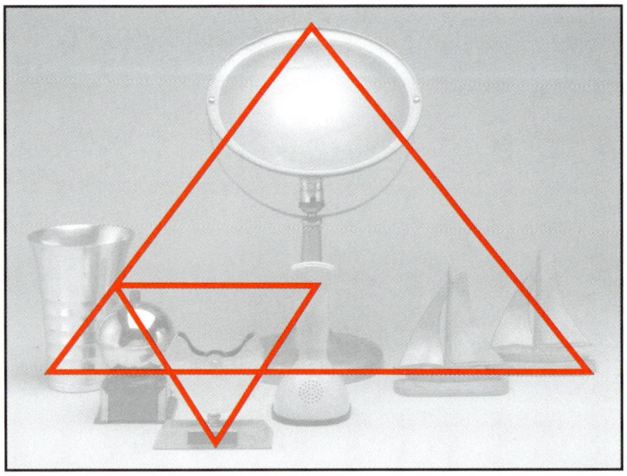

From left; English Kaymet anodized aluminum vase, c.1945, $150-175. American Smokador Hi-Ball ashtray/cigarette box, c.1940, $250-300. English Aspreys chrome and shagreen match holder, c.1935, $200-250. American North Electric Ericofon desk phone, c.1960, $100-120. Canadian unmarked adjustable shade industrial lamp, c.1940, $300-325. American Bronzart figural yacht bookends, c.1930, $125-175.

From front; English unmarked geometric enamel compact, c.1935, $100-150. English unmarked green Bakelite compact, c.1939, $275-300. American unmarked giant green enamel compact, c.1935, $100-150. Pair of English FoFrame chrome and enamel post-card frames, c.1930, $275-300. Pair of English unmarked chrome and Bakelite twin candleholders, c.1935, $275-300. English unmarked hand painted geometric ceramic and chrome pillar lamp, c.1935, $300-400.

CIRCULAR BAKELITE and enamel compacts placed in an ascending row lead the eye towards a tall geometric ceramic fluted column shaped lamp. Symmetrically placed FoFrames and chrome and green marbled Bakelite candleholders complete the arrangement.

A LARGE hand carved wooden Zulu warrior bust looks down on a presentation Kodak 1-A camera and box designed by Walter Dorwin Teague. the rich colors of the wood in the bust are picked up by the English candlesticks in the foreground and by the painted faux grain on the chrome triple candleholders in the rear.

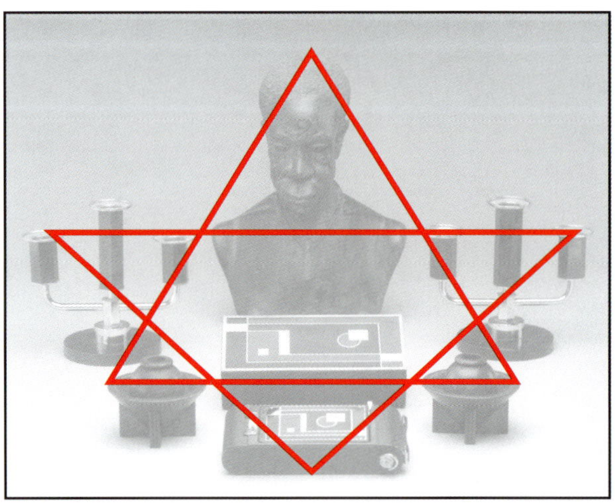

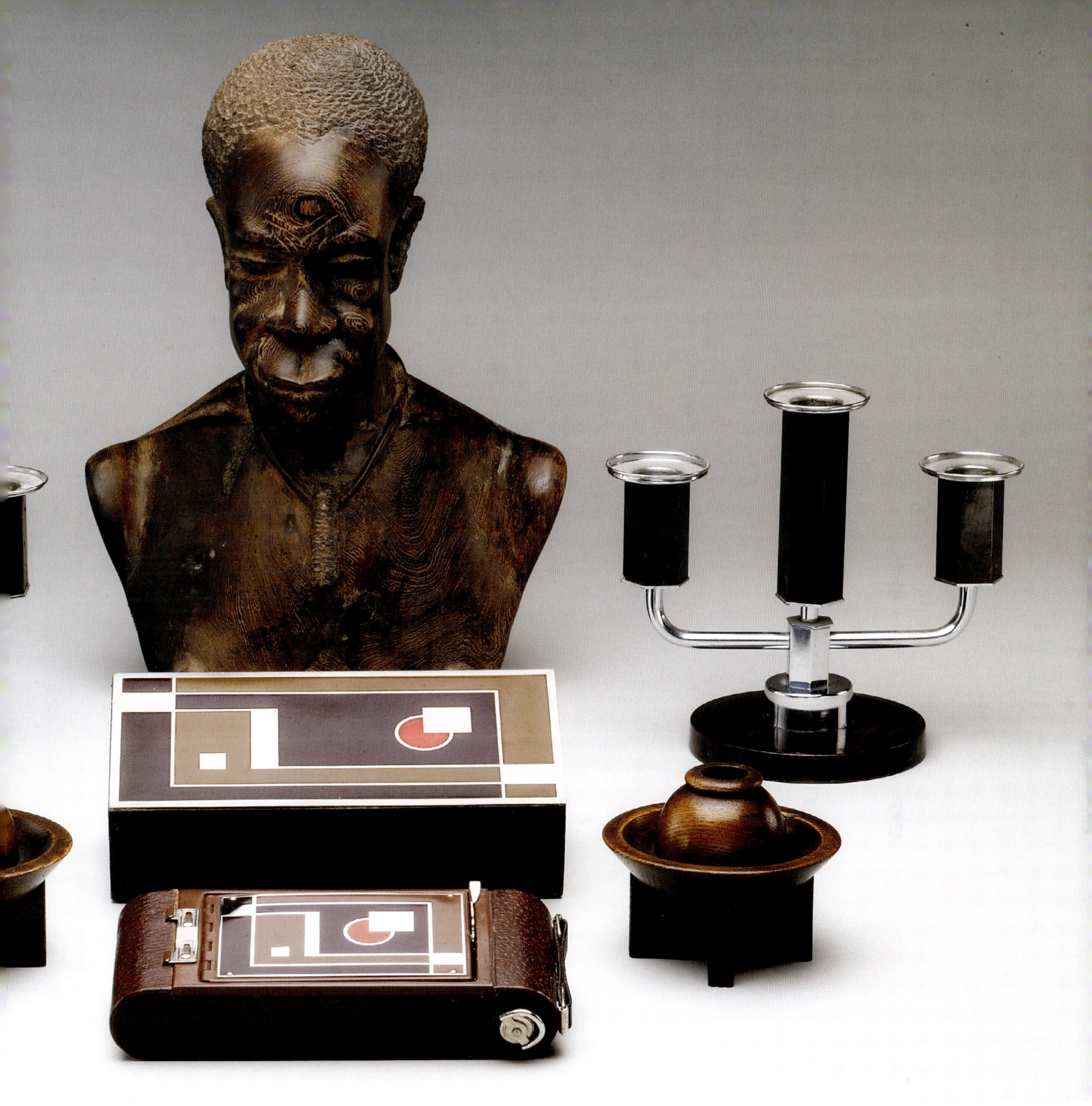

Clockwise from left: pair of English hand-turned wood candlesticks by Ebenezer Gomme c.1930, $150-175. Pair of Belgian unmarked triple candle holders, c.1930, $275-325. African unmarked hand carved "airport art" bust, c.1955, $325-350. American Kodak 1-A camera with box by Walter Dorwin Teague, c.1935, $750-850.

A GERMAN inlaid wood figural cigar box is here surrounded by an American Town Crier cocktail shaker and glasses, plus two color coordinated geometric bud vases. The three table lighters, from Japan, Germany and England respectively, are placed at an angle in front of this otherwise very symmetrical group.

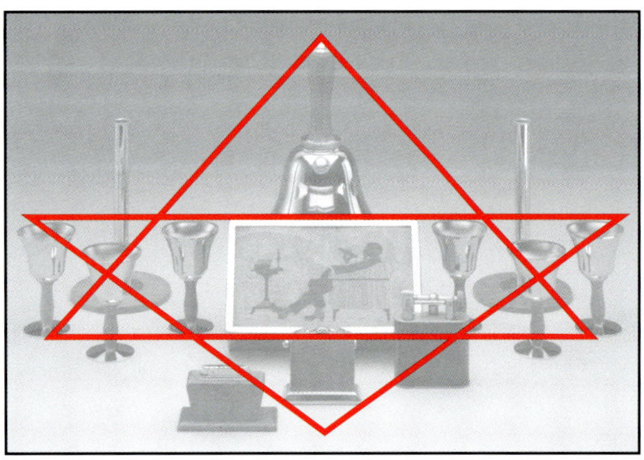

Clockwise from left: American Town Crier seven piece cocktail set, c.1942, $750-850. Pair of American unmarked bud vases, c.1940, $125-175. English Jumbo silver plated wheel and flint table lighter, c.1930, $200-250. German Kashie wheel and flint table lighter, c.1955, $125-170. American Bentley wheel and flint table lighter, c.1942, $100-125. German unmarked figural marquetry and chrome cigar box, c.1929, $800-900.

T HIS GROUP celebrates five decades of appreciation of the female form, from the kitsch to the elegant. Centred by the large plaster figure from the 20's and bounded by the etched pocket flasks from the 60's, this is a very themed and classic arrangement.

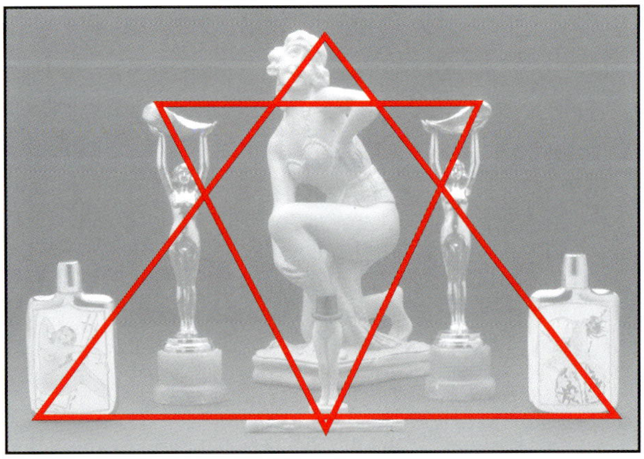

Clockwise from left: Pair of Japanese unmarked figural nude hip flasks, c.1965, $150-175 each. Pair of French Limousin feather dancer statuettes, c.1925, $750-850. American painted plaster statue, c.1929, $400-450. Japanese plastic figural nude ball-point pen, c.1965, $50-75. American Negbaur Miss Cutie table lighter, c.1940, $100-125.

A GROUPING of stunningly designed Zeiss Ikon desk barometers, with the centre one being accessorized with the Lufft temperature gauge fitted to the top. These classic objects are arranged in a very simple layout to show their beautiful design to maximum effect.

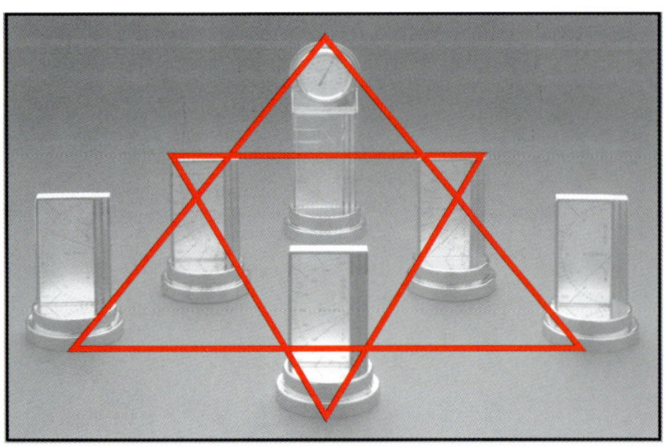

This collection of German Zeiss Ikon desk barometers dates from the thirties. they were made for both export and domestic use, $750-850 each. In centre complete with Lufft attachement, $850-950.

A VANITY grouping that centres on a hand painted ABCO plaster figurine and a yellow Lucite and chrome vanity tray, which is placed vertically to provide a backdrop for the grouping. The geometric forms of the black Bakelite brush and mirror complement the black sides of the yellow and clear Lucite of the English dressing table accessory set.

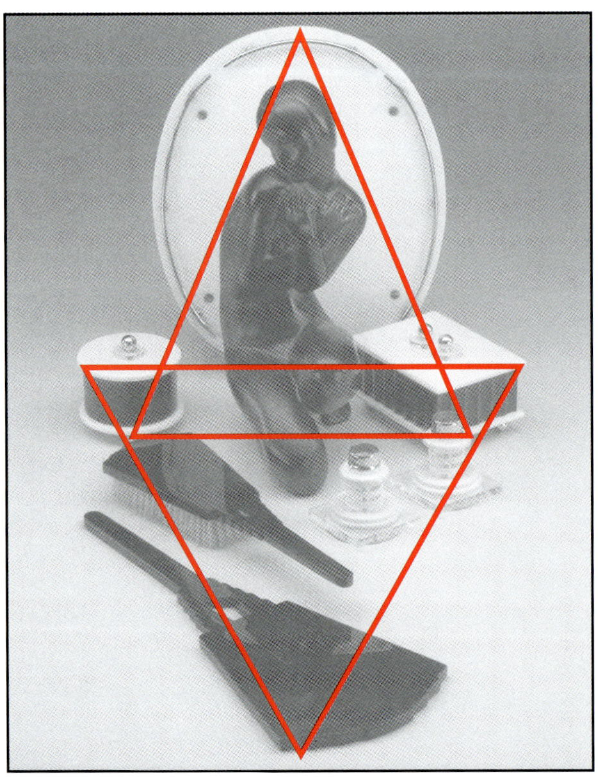

Clockwise from left: English unmarked Lucite and Bakelite dressing table box, c.1939, $150-175. English unmarked chrome and Lucite vanity tray, c.1939, $100-125. English unmarked Lucite and Bakelite cigarette box, c.1938, $200-225. Pair oif English unmarked Lucite and chrome candlesticks, c.1939, $200-225. American La Futuriste Bakelite brush and mirrir set by NTS, c.1930 $375-425. American ABCO painted plaster statuette, c.1950, $200-225.

A THEMED grouping of Phenolic resin accented nut birds with an American Catalin pigeon racing trophy in the rear. The ashtray in the foreground is from France, while the remaining nut birds were originally produced for Dunhill by the YZ Company of England.

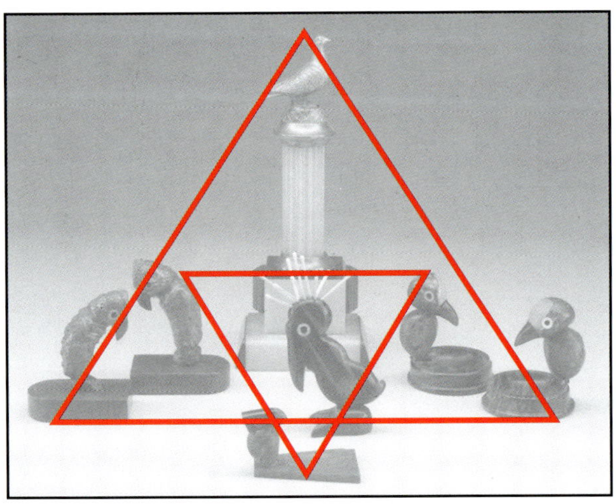

Clockwise from left: Pair of English YZ nutbird bookends, c.1930, $700-800. American unmarked Catalin pigeon racing trophy, c.1949, $400-500. Pair of English YZ nutbird ashtrays, c.1930, $800-900. French unmarked nutbird ashtray, c.1930, $200-250. English YZ nutbird match holder/striker, c.1930, $200-250.

THE DARK RED of the Bakelite clock forms a visual centre for this group, with the two diagonal boudoir lamps leading the eye to it. The large photograph in the rear gives a balance of height to this very symmetrical arrangement.

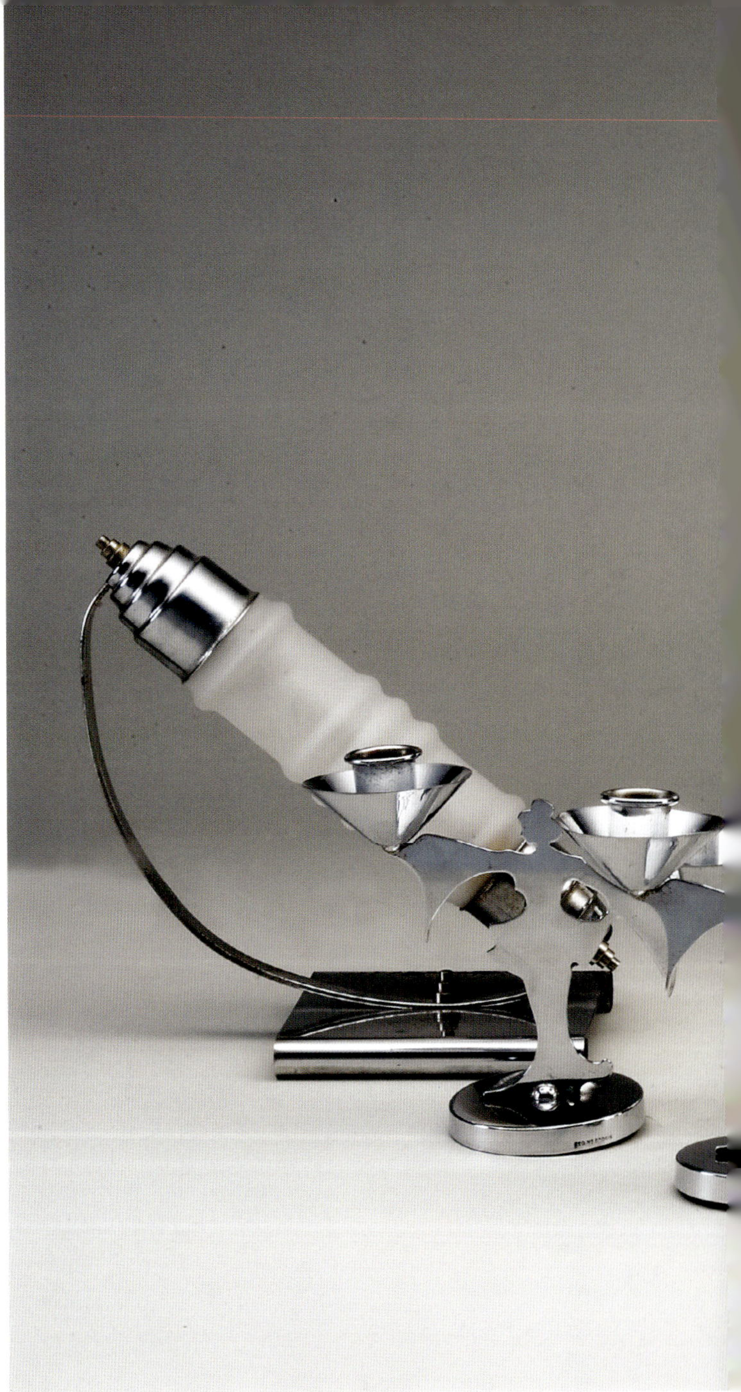

Clockwise from left: Pair of American unmarked frosted glass and chrome boudoir lights, c.1936, $450-500. English Staybright chrome photo-frame, c.1930, $275-300. German unmarked desk clock/barometer combination, c.1935, $250-275. French CH miniature desk weather station, c.1930, $175-200. Pair of English unmarked figural twin candleholders, c.1936, $200-250. German unmarked Bakelite veneered mechanical clock, c.1939, $275-300.

VERTICAL TUBULAR SHAPES form the premiere design theme for this arrangement; from the dinner gong to the lighters, to the candlesticks they create a strong vertical structure. To balance this out they are interspersed with the strong circular shapes of the Art Deco nutcrackers and the stylized figurative accent lamp designed by Helen Dryden for Revere that holds the foreground.

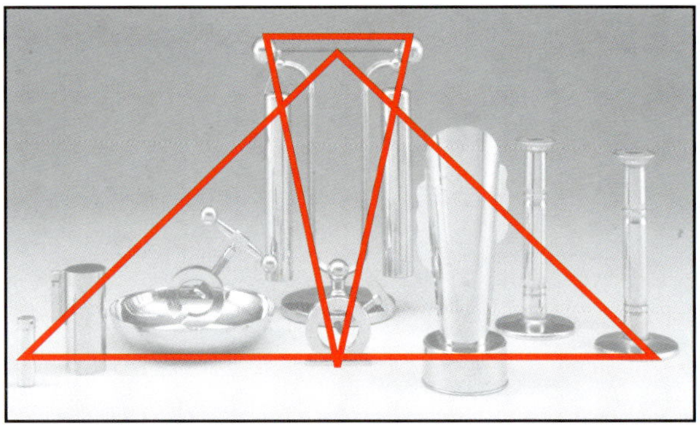

From left: American unmarked aluminum wheel and flint lighter, c.1942, $75-100. French Jury butane table lighter, c.1960, $150-175. English unmarked nutcracker and dish combination, c.1939, $175-225. American unmarked dinner gong, c.1935, $275-325. English nunmarked nutcracker, c.1930, $100-125. American Revere figural accent lamp, c.1936, $550-650. Pair of English unmarked chrome candlesticks, c.1939, $175-200.

These French unmarked chrome and wood photo-frames date from the early thirties, 2½"x3½, $95-110, 3½"x5¾", $125-150, 5"x7", $150-175, 8"x10", $175-225. Australian unmarked chrome and wood candlesticks, c.1935, $225-275.

COMPLEMENTARY angled chrome shapes and dark wood feature in this grouping, which-combines several sizes of French photo frames from the 20's with a similarly styled pair of geometrically bold candlesticks from Australia.

THE COMPLEMENTARY tones of green celluloid, phenolic and Bakelite are combined with chrome in this grouping, which is based largely on circular motifs. A pair of clay nude statuettes by Foley are placed on either edge at an angle and thus serve to bookend the wings of this arrangement.

Clockwise from center: German unmarked Celluloid desk clock, c.1935, $225-275. Pair of English unmarked chrome and Bakelite candlesticks, c.1935. $225-275. English unmarked marbled Bakelite postcard frame, c.1936, $120-130. Pair of Canadian plaster figural bookends by B. Foley, c.1936, $500-550. English unmarked chrome figural dinner gong, c.1935, $250-275. English unmarked green Bakelite postcard frame, c.1936, $120-130. English unmarked Bakelite and chrome barometer/perpetual calendar combination, c.1930, $250-275.

THIS GROUP OF sympathetically designed electrical and mechanical clocks was produced in England by a variety of manufacturers and in a wide variety of materials. This arrangement would be ideal for a mantle piece or long table, and in this case is illuminated by a Canadian classic bronze metal and chrome tiered lamp by Crown.

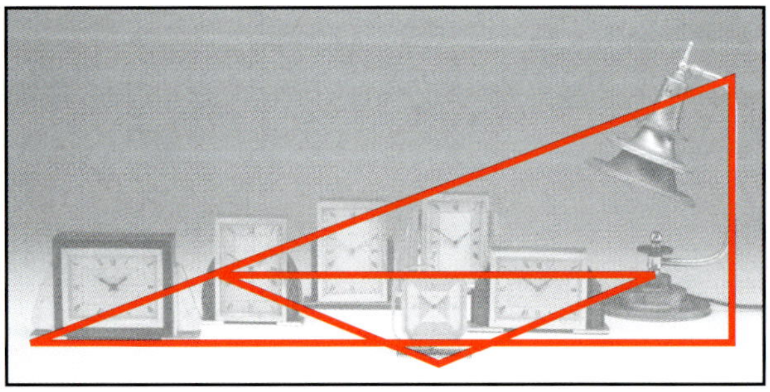

From left: English Temco chrome and wood electric mantle clock, c.1936, $275-325. English Widex chrome and carved oak mechanical clock, c.1936, $300-375. English unmarked chrome and Bakelite mechanical clock, c.1936, $300-375. English unmarked chrome and wood veneer mechanical mantle clock, c.1936, $275-350. Canadian Crown tiered desk lamp, c.1935, $650-750. English unmarked chrome and Bakelite mechanical mantle clock, c.1936, $300-375. English Perivale chrome swivel clock, c.1935, $200-250.

BOUNDED BY two magnificent Art Deco weather stations by Lufft, this grouping features items from England, Germany, France and Japan. All of these examples date from the 30's and 40's, save for the Lucite Sputnik in the rear which is from the 60's.

Clockwise from left: English Unigraph desk weather station and perpetual calendar, c.1936, $850-950. German Lufft brass and enamel weather station, c.1940, $350-450. German Lufft Sputnik chrome and plastic weather station, c.1960, $175-250. German Lufft brass and enamel weather station, c.1940, $350-450. German Lufft desktop barometer and hygrometer, c.1945, $550-650. English Joseph Lucas desktop thermometer by Rototherm, c.1950, $100-150. French unmarked miniature chrome barometer, c.1935, $100-125. In center: French Lancel/Lufft clock weather station in copper and steel, c.1930, $850-950.

THE RICH HUES of natural wood dominate this grouping, and from the obviously home made Trench Art frame and book ends in the foreground to the copper, wood, and parchment boudoir lamps in the back, these pieces exude an overall warmth.

Clockwise from center: Canadian unmarked Trench Art photo-frame, c.1944, $75-100. American Revere book holder with West Therm barometer by Fred Farr, c.1940, $175-200. American Airguide desk barometer, c.1942, $125-150. American United two-tone wood electric mantle clock, c.1939, $100-450. Pair of Canadian unmarked copper and wood bed-side lights, c.1945, $175-225. American Pla-Wood pipe humidor, c.1940, $250-275. French unmarked glass and wood candy box, c.1935, $275-300. Canadian unmarked Outsider Art geometric bookends, c.1935, $150-175.

THIS GROUPING OF Tobacciana is bounded by two almost matching adjustable chrome accent lamps from America. The group features a nude silhouette ashtray from New Zealand, a swan pipe rack with pipes, and an ashtray cigarette box combination from America, plus an English novelty cigarette box with a Bakelite topped large chrome and brass ash receiver.

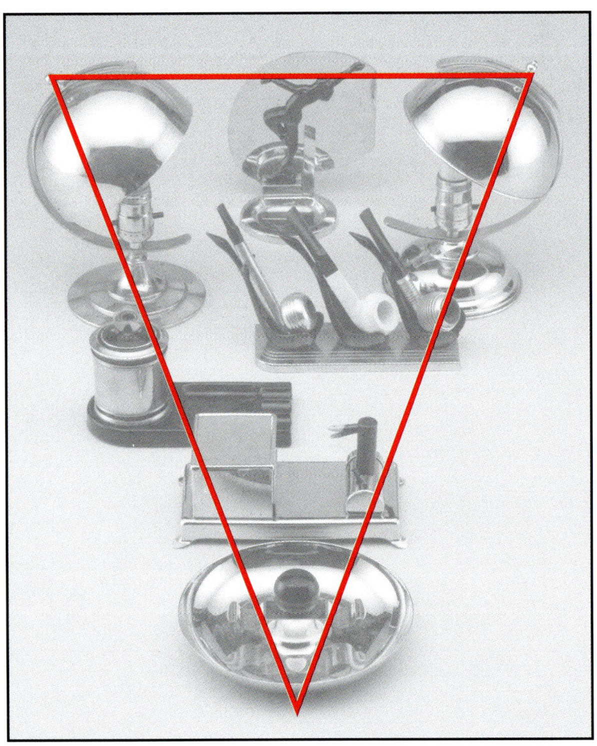

From front: American unmarked chrome and Bakelite gear knob ashtray, c.1945, $100-125. English unmarked figural automatic cigarette box, c.1935, $250-275. American Park Sherman cigarette box/ashtray combination, c.1935, $100-125. American Die Casters of New York figural swan pipe rack, c.1935, $200-275. American unmarked adjustable shade lamp with stepped base, c.1935, $225-275. New Zealand unmarked chrome and enamel figural nude ashtray, c.1935, $275-300. American unmarked adjustable shade lamp with domed base, c.1935, $225-275.

AN AMERICAN desk lamp looks over a Scottish clock, a German clock, and an English calendar striker lighter. This symmetrical grouping is bounded on the sides by a pair of American biomorphic silver plated candleholders from the 50's, a pair of adjustable flashlights from the 40's and a classically designed pair of Braun table lighters from the 60's.

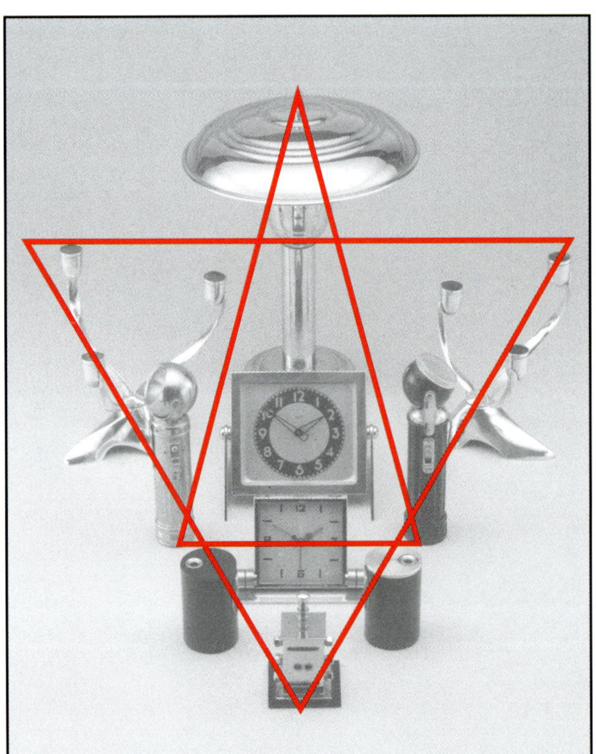

From front: English unmarked perpetual calendar/touch tip tablelighter combination, c.1930, $350-375. German Braun black butane table lighter by Dieter Ram, c.1968, $100-150. German Braun black and chrome butane table lighter by Dieter Ram, c.1968, $100-150. Italian unmarked chrome alarm clock, c.1935, $325-350. Indian Train swivel head flashlight, c.1945, $75-100. Scottish Glen chrome mechanical desk clock, c.1939, $270-300. American USALITE black plastic and chrome swivel head flashlight, c.1950, $75-100. Pair of American Reed Barton silver plated triple candleholders. c.1953, $500-525. Canadian unmarked chrome table lamp, c.1939, $250-275.

GLEN

THIS GROUP OF eccentrically decorated enamelled glass cocktail pieces was almost certainly produced originally for the French market but manufactured in Czechoslovakia. The darker color of the smaller cocktail glasses on the right balances the larger clear glass pieces on the left.

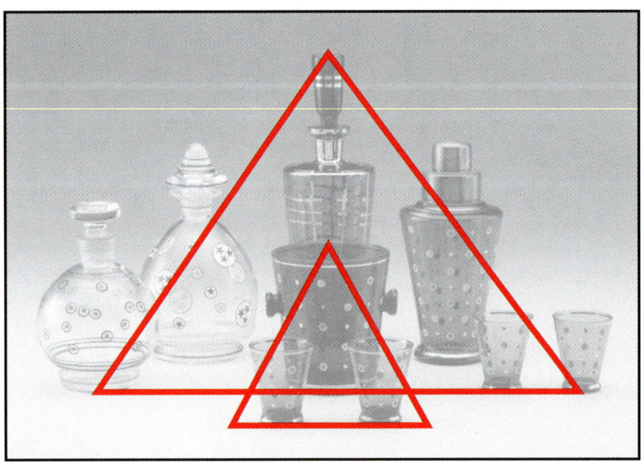

Clockwise from left: Czechoslovakian unmarked black and red enamelled decanter, c.1945, $300-350. Czechoslovakian unmarked black and white enamelled decanter, c.1945, $300-350. Czechoslovakian unmarked red and mirrored enamelled decanter, c.1945, $300-350. Czechoslovakian unmarked polychrome and gilt enamelled six piece cocktail set, c.1939, $325-375.

A VERY GRAPHICALLY designed Movado clock fronts this musically inspired red and black grouping. The plaster dancing flapper in the centre is framed by two figural musician lamps from postwar Germany. The bisque four piece band is also from Germany, while the red based chrome picture frames are from England.

From front: Swiss Movado desk clock, c.1930, $675-775. German unmarked four piece bisque jazz band, c.1935, $250-300. American unmarked Bakelite and plastic boxed poker chips, c.1945, $150-200. Pair of English unmarked chrome and red enamel postcard frames, c.1935, $250-300. American unmarked painted plaster flapper statuette, c.1929. $300-400. Pair of West German unmarked musician lamps, c.1946, $1750-2000.

TWO LARGE Art Deco brass altar candlesticks stand either side of a massive floral twin table lamp believed to be from Israel. Two hand painted ginger jars and a pair of Belgian triple candle-holders are fronted by two English female statuettes

From front: English Bacci and Bacci plaster figurine, c.1935, $225-250. French unmarked plaster figurine on marble base, c.1929, $250-300. Pair of Belgian unmarked brass triple candleholders, c.1930, $325-375. Pair of English unmarked hand painted ginger jars, c.1930, $1000-1500. Pair of Canadian unmarked brass altar candlesticks, c.1940, $500-550. Israeli (?) unmarked double console lamp, c.1939, $1200-1500.

THESE TWO groupings are of wonderfully colorful Faience ceramics from Provence that all date from the 30's and were produced by the Faience de St. Jean

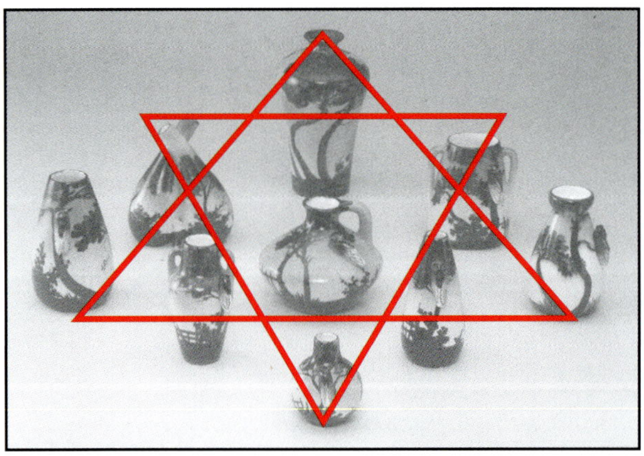

du Desert and hand painted by L. Berty. Arrangements of this French pottery always display well, owing to its extremely vibrant palette.

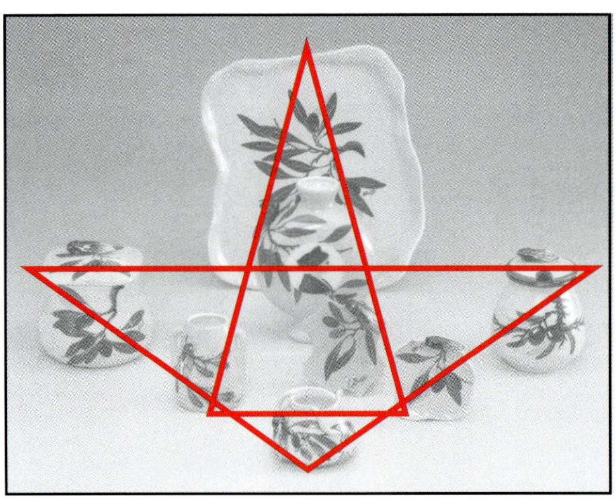

French Faience de St. Jean du Desert hand painted by L. Berty and dating from the twenties to the forties with a price range of $125 -$525.

TWO PLASTER ladies seem to dance in gay abandon around the amusingly designed three part console table lamp set, while the English green mirrored clock in the centre serves to hold the grouping together visually.

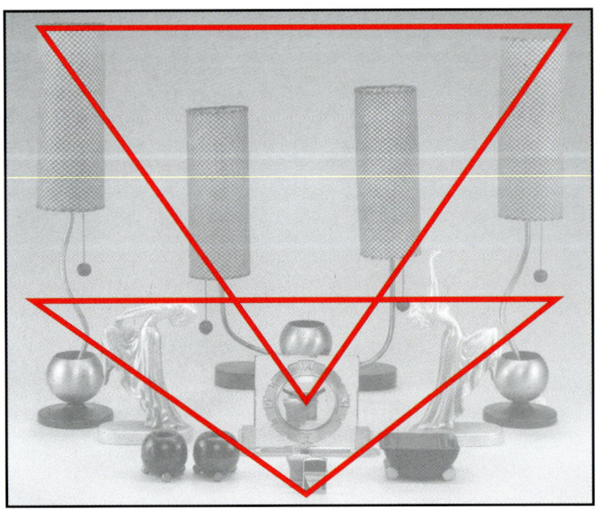

From front: Japanese Ritz advertising wheel and flint pocket lighter, c.1950, $75-100. American ASR wheel and flint table lighter, c.1945, $75-100. Pair of American Nelson ball candlesticks, c.1955, $100-125. English Bristol Bakelite and brass cigarette box, c.1935, $375-400. English Smiths brass and and mirror electric mantle clock, c.1936, $275-300. Pair of American unmarked painted plaster dancing figures, c.1940, $350-400. Set of three Canadian unmarked flower vase/console lamps, c.1958, $275-375.

Clockwise from left: American unmarked silver plate and Bakelite coffee set, c.1935, $1750-2000. American unmarked chrome table lamp, c.1942, $600-650. Czechoslovakian Moffem desk lamp/clock combination, c.1939, $1200-1500. French unmarked marble photo-frame, c.1929, $125-150. English unmarked triple candleholder, c.1935, $125-150. English Smiths chrome and glass barometer, c.1936, $150-175. English Craftsmen mechanical mantle clock, c.1935, $325-375.

THE HIGH END

three piece coffee set on the left is balanced by the rare Moffem clock lamp, triple candleholder and marble based photo frame on the other side, while the American chrome lamp, English mantle clock and barometer form a strong central line for the arrangement.

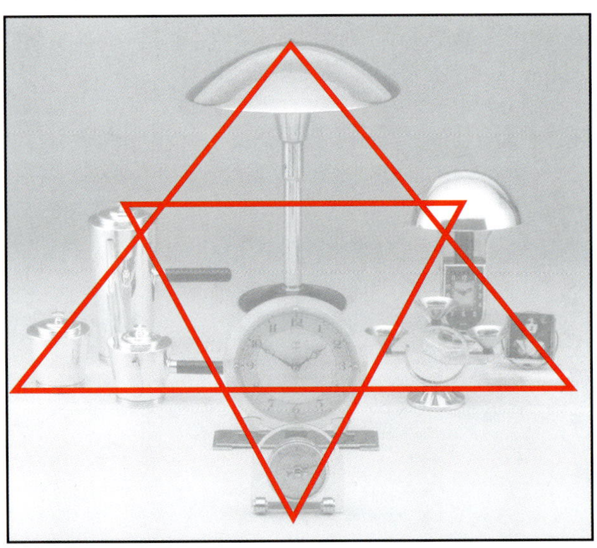

8 DAY
Change
RAIN
FAIR
Stormy
Very Dry

From front: Set of six English unmarked Lucite napkin rings, c.1945, $125-150. English unmarked Lucite Toast rack, c.1945, $100-125. Pair of English unmarked Lucite spill vases, c.1939, $175-200. English unmarked Lucite cake stand, c.1945, $175-225. English unmarked chrome table lamp with Lucite shade, c.1939, $750-850.

HERE A GROUPING of predominantly peachy pink Lucite English table items is placed in a strictly symmetrical arrangement. The two spill vases, although of slightly different size and shape, work together well as a result of the somewhat formal layout.

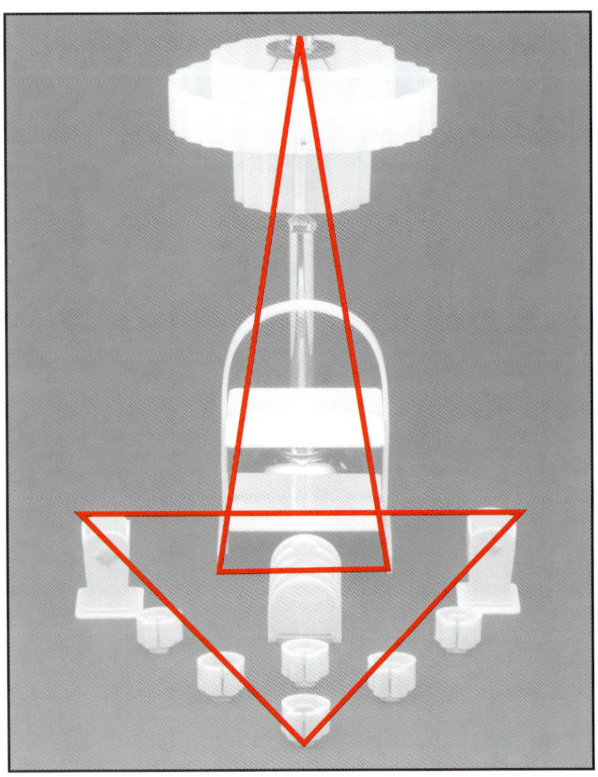

A FORMAL arrangement of a Susie Cooper Tango banded part coffee set. The iconic Kestrel coffee pot is placed with four coffee cans and saucers on an English anodized Kaymet tray in the centre of the grouping.

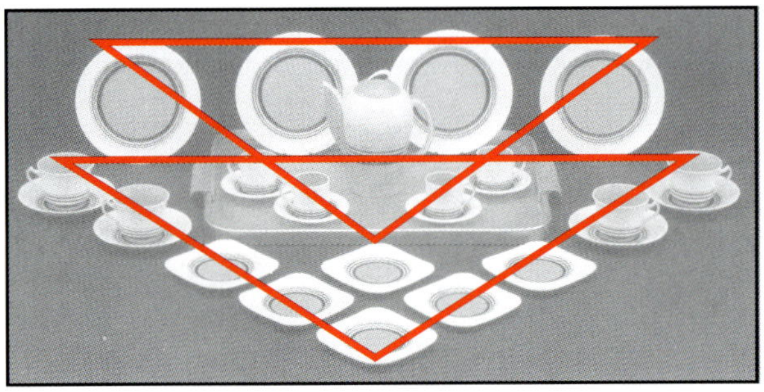

English Kaymet anodized aluminum tray, c.1945, $125-150. English Tango ceramic coffee items by Susie Cooper, c.1939: coffee cans and saucers $100-150 each, tea cups and saucers, $100-125 each, set of six square plates, $400-450, set of four side plates, $400-425, Kestrel coffee pot, $200-300.

From front: Japanese unmarked wheel and flint figural airplane table lighter, c.1935, $250-275. Japanese unmarked wheel and flint figural airplane table lighter, c.1942, $250-275. German unmarked figural airplane complete cocktail set, c.1930, $15,000-18,000. German unmarked figural airplane complete smokers set, c.1930, $7000-9000. German unmarked figural Zeppelin complete cocktail set, c.1930, $4000-5000.

THIS GROUPING with an aviation theme features three icons of German Art Deco design of the 30's: The Zeppelin cocktail shaker, the airplane cocktail set, and the airplane smoker's companion. They are here displayed with a pair of Japanese airplane table lighters from a slightly later date.

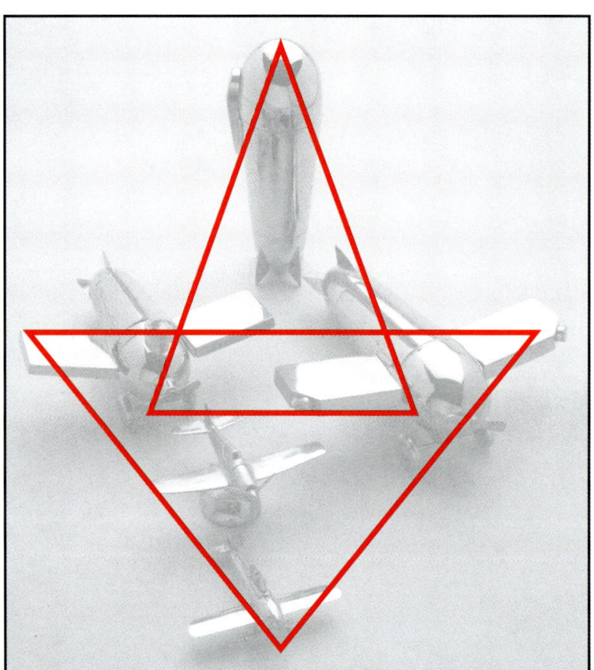

THE TRIANGULAR shade of the large Peruvian brass skyscraper table lamp dictates the shaping of this group and the items below follow the lines created by it. A counter diagonal row of clocks leads the eye back to the centre of the arrangement.

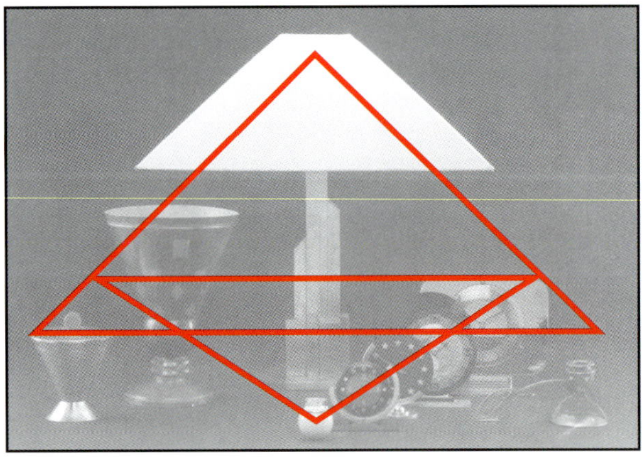

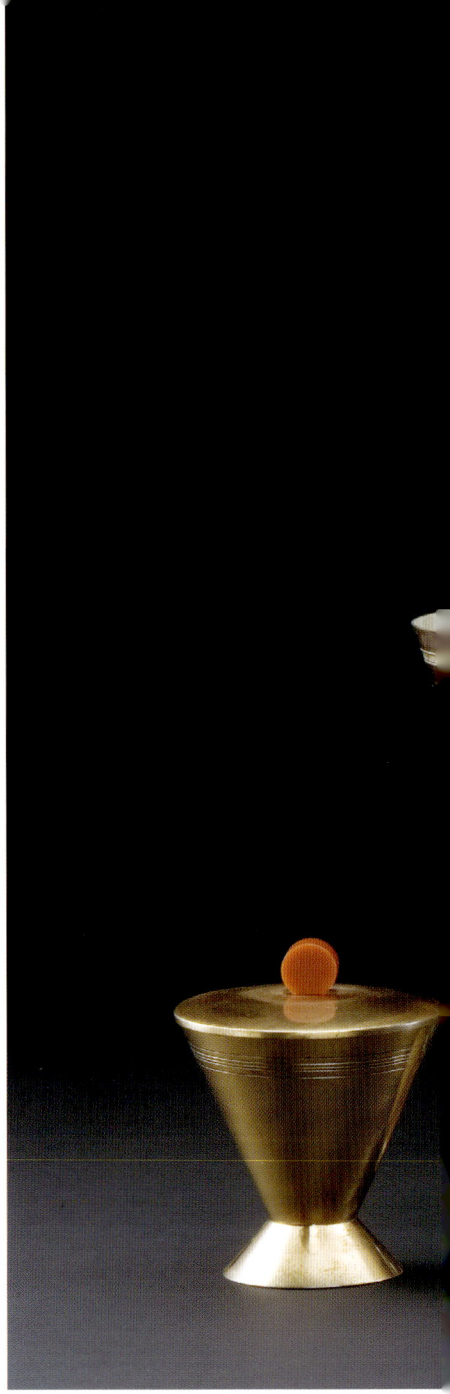

Clockwise from left: American Benedict covered vase, c.1929, $100-150. French unmarked table torchiere, c.1923, $1750-2000. Peruvian brass skyscraper lamp, c.1930, $200-2500. English Smiths mirror and brass mechanical clock, c.1939, $400-450. English unmarked mechanical picture clock, c.1935, $375-450. American Seth Thomas Bakelite and brass mechanical desk clock, c.1935, $225-275. German unmarked Jugenstil chamber stick, c.1905, $175-225. American plastic and metal mechanical desk clock, c.1949, $125-150. German unmarked wheel and flint Bakelite ball table lighter, c.1939, $150-175.

PAIRS OF items balance each other on both sides of this almost totally symmetrical arrangement, with perhaps the only exeption being the figural nude clock in the centre rear. Even the vibrant colors of the Catalin Mahjong counters are stacked symmetrically on their rack in the foreground.

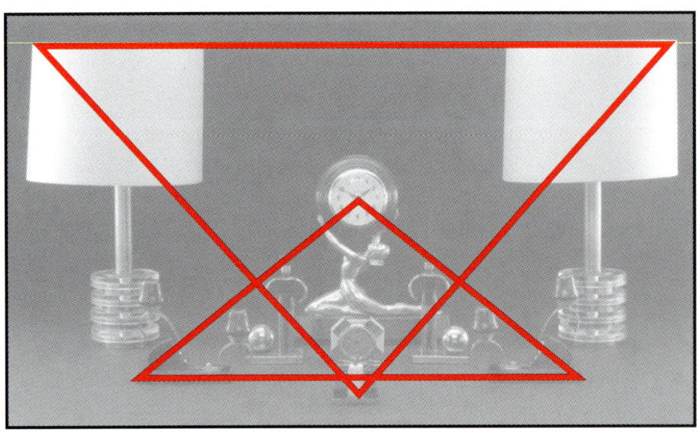

From front: American unmarked Catalin Mahjong counter set, c.1939, $125-150. Pair of Belgian unmarked twin candleholders, c.1940, $175-225. German unmarked celluloid mechanical clock, c.1930, $150-175. Pair of American Chase Sentinel bookends, c.1938, $625-675. Pair of American unmarked brass and glass console lamps, c.1930, $1500-2000. Canadian Snyder figural nude mechanical mantle clock, c.1939, $450-475.

A LARGE English black and white Lucite mantle clock holds the centre of this group while the diagonal arm of the Site Lite desk lamp bounds the left hand edge and is in turn paralleled by the diagonal row of lighters, compacts and a frame on the right.

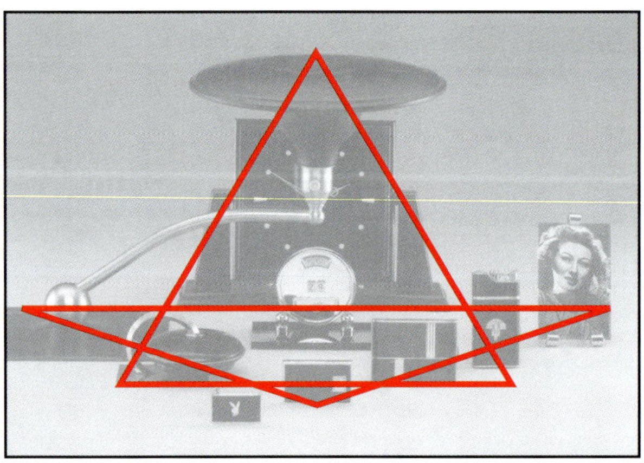

Clockwise from left: Canadian Site Lite desk lamp, c.1945, $375-425. English Smiths Bakelite and Lucite electric mantle clock, c.1945, $325-350. French unmarked chrome postcard frame, c.1935, $175-200. American Evans wheel and flint lighter/cigarette case combination, c.1939, $200-250. American Evans cigarette case, c.1939, $150-175. German unmarked watch compact, c.1945, $200-225. American Playboy wheel and flint pocket lighter, c.1960, $75-100. English unmarked vanity table compact, c.1935, $200-225. English unmarked chrome and Bakelite perpetual desk calendar, c.1935, $175-200.

BLACK, RED AND silver tones link this grouping of smoking and drinking items all together. The bold patterning and design of the large Ritz Thermos cocktail shaker thoroughly anchors the group, while the four enamelled ashtrays are placed vertically in a row and conversely anchor the group horizontally.

From front: Pair of American unmarked enamelled sterling match box covers, c.1930, $75-100. Japanese unmarked wheel and flint lighter/ashtray set, c.1942, $125-150. Set of four American unmarked enamelled sterling ashtrays, c.1930, $175-200. Set of six Japanese liqueur glasses, c.1946, $200-250. Japanese Hudson wheel and flint lighter/cigarette case combination, c.1942, $175-200. American Ritz Bakelite and chrome Thermos cocktail shaker, c.1939, $275-325.

AWK
AWK
AWK
AWK
AWK
AWK

THE STRONG VERTICALS of the upright Gyrobar are softened by the curved lines of the Chase Taurex candleholders. The geometric lines of the high Art Deco mirror and brush that are placed at right angles lead one's eye into the other objects in the arrangement.

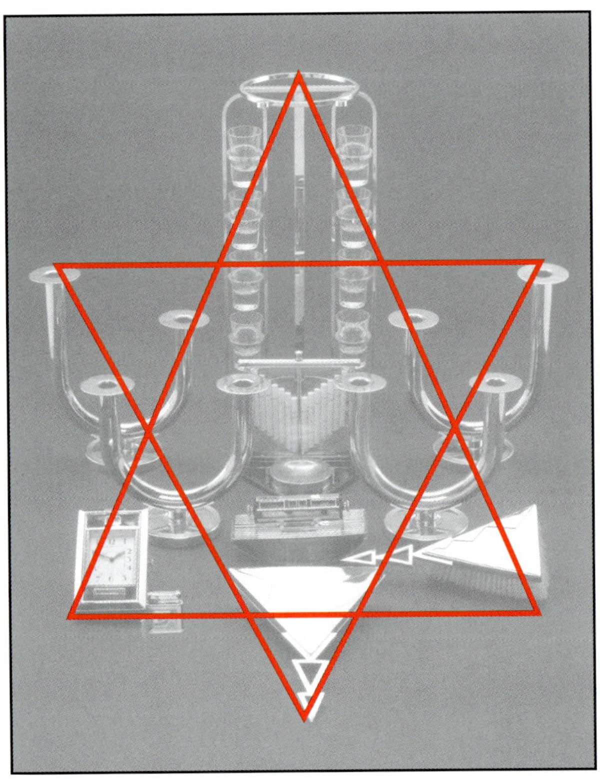

Clockwise from left: American Colibri picture wheel and flint pocket lighter, c.1942, $150-175. German unmarked perpetual calendar/clock/desk blotter combination, c.1935, $275-325. Pair of American Chase Taurex Even candleholders by Walter Von Nessen, c.1936, $375-400. Pair of American Taurex Uneven candleholders, by Walter Von Nesson, c.1936, $375-400. American unmarked gyroscopic yacht bar, c.1935, $550-600. French unmarked geometric brush and mirror set, c.1926, $1250-1750. English unmarked perpetual calendar/desk blotter combination, c.1935, $250-275. German unmarked table cigarette dispenser/ashtray combination, c.1936, $200-250.

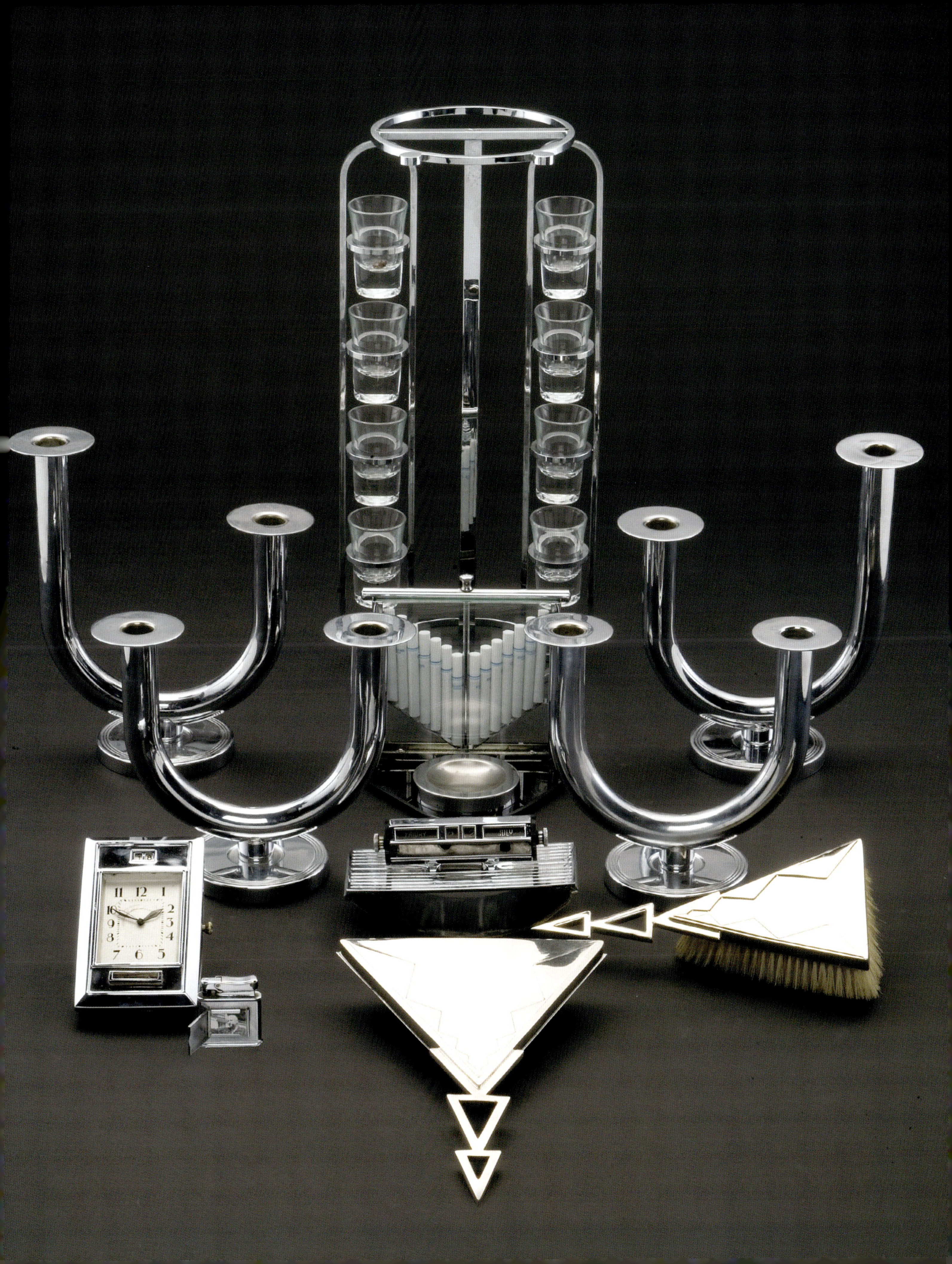

CLEAR LUCITE accented with red is used to great effect in the large Canadian lamp and the American highly patriotic twin picture frame. Two English and one American clear Lucite clocks are bounded on each side by a pair of American Manhattan glass vases and in front by a Canadian clear Lucite cigarette box.

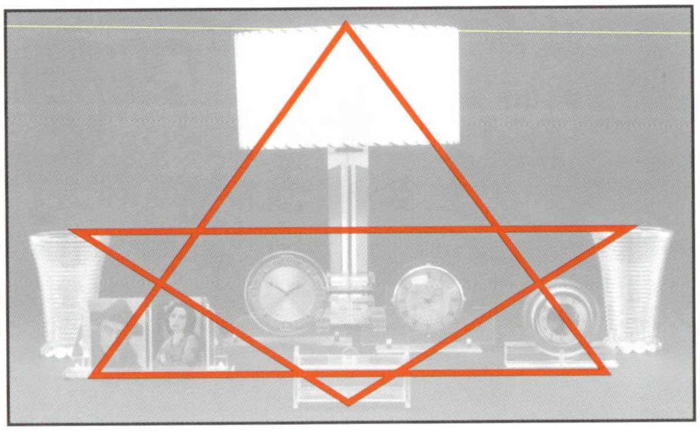

Clockwise from center: Canadian unmarked Lucite cigarette box, c.1939, $100-125. American unmarked tri-color Lucite twin photo-frame, c.1945, $125-150. Pair of American Manhattan vases, c.1939, $100-150. English unmarked Lucite mechanical mantle clock, c.1939, $225-250. Canadian unmarked Lucite table lamp, c.1935, $500-550.English Smiths Lucite mechanical desk clock, c.1945, $200-225. American Seth Thomas Lucite electric table clock, c.1942, $175-200.

THE HAND PAINTED pink and black tones of the large ABCO figural lamp are reflected in the pink and black Lucite of the French clock and the English candleholders and photo frame below the black silk shade. the pair of angled 50's electric table lighters lead the eye into the group, while the Bakelite KEM playing card box anchors the group in the foreground.

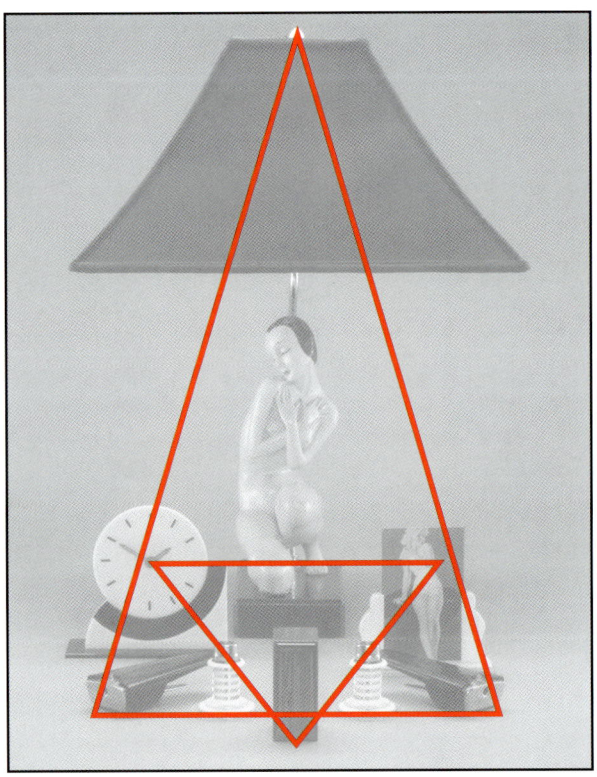

Clockwise from left: French unmarked Lucite and Bakelite electric desk clock, c.1939, $325-350. American ABCO figural painted plaster table lamp, c.1950, $400-425. English unmarked Lucite postcard frame c.1945, $150-175. Pair of American unmarked wheel and flint table lighters, c.1956, $120-150. Pair of English unmarked Lucite and chrome candlesticks, c.1939, $225-275. American KEM Bakelite playing card box, c.1935, $100-125.

BLONDE WOOD, solid black and brass colors form the theme for this eccentric grouping. The bizarre dog sculpture on the right blends in with both the Israeli mantle clock in the centre and the French photo frames on the left. While the Italian brass cocktail shaker and jigger and the bizarre table lighter in front are both from the 60's, the sunburst lamp dates from the 40's.

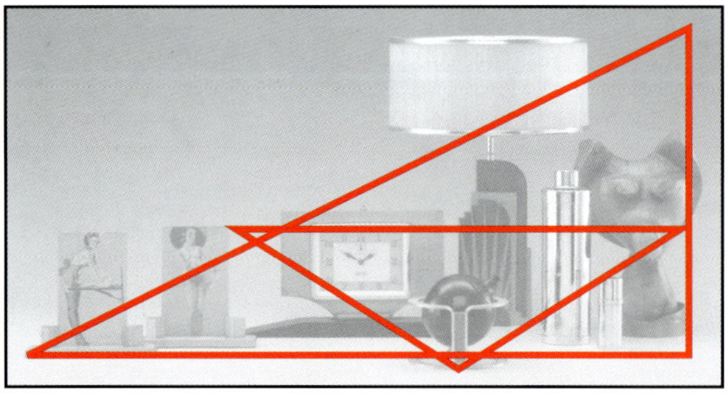

From left: Pair of French unmarked wooden postcard frames, c.1930, $175-200. Israeli Idox wood mechanical alarm clock, c.1946, $275-300. Japanese unmarked electric touch tip table lighter, c.1965, $100-125. Canadian unmarked Outsider Art marquetry table lamp, c.1945, $325-350. Italian unmarked brass cocktail shaker and jigger, c.1958, $200-225. American unmarked brass and wood Found Art dog sculpture, c.1955, $300-325.

IN THIS NAUTICALLY themed grouping, a small flotilla of Bakelite and chrome ship shaped cruets and table lighters from England and Japan sail information from an American incredibly detailed lighthouse shaped cocktail shaker.

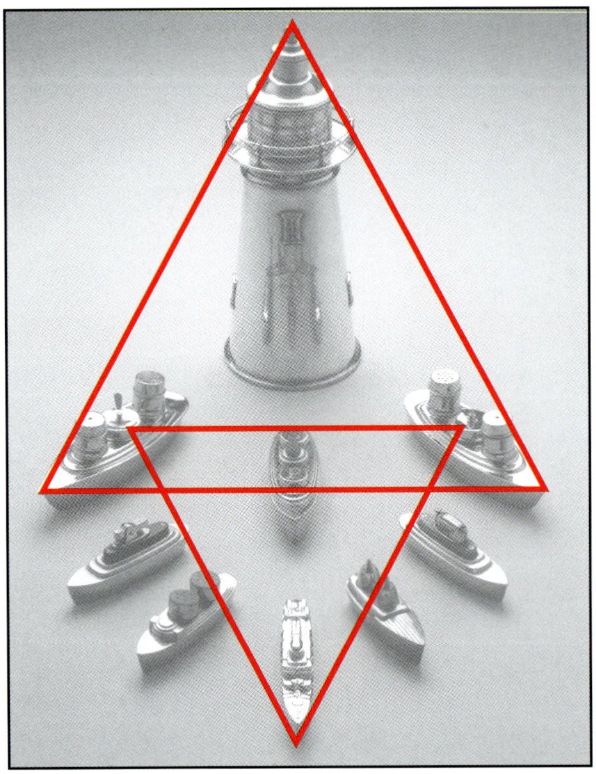

Clockwise from front: Japanese unmarked wheel and flint figural ship table lighter, c.1955, $100-125. Japanese unmarked red plastic and chrome cruet set, c.1940, $125-150. Japanese unmarked black Bakelite and chrome wheel and flint figural ship table lighter, c.1942, $150-175. English unmarked chrome four piece figural ship cruet set, c.1939, $250-275. American unmarked figural lighthouse cocktail shaker, c.1929, $8000-12,000. English unmarked chrome four piece figural ship cruet set, c.1939, $250-275. Japanese unmarked red plastic and chrome wheel and flint table lighter, c.1940, $125-150. Japanese unmarked three piece figural ship cruet set, c.1935, $125-150. In center: English unmarked chrome and red Bakelite four piece figural ship cruet set, c.1935, $200-250.

WHILE TODAY this grouping would definitely be considered politically incorrect, in the time that these items were made they were considered highly fashionable, whether they were diner and smoking accessories or highly priced French perfume bottles.

Clockwise from front: American Coon Chicken Inn matchbook, c.1940, $45-55. American Coon Chicken Inn cigarette dispenser, c.1935, $750-850. American Ronson bartender smokers set, c.1939, $2750-3750. American unmarked brass and wood Bell-hop cigarette pack and match holder, c.1935, $250-350. French Golliwog perfume bottlle by Vigny, c.1930, $950-1050. French Golliwog Jack, Jill and Junior boxed perfume bottle set, c.1930, $1250-1350. American Coon Chicken Inn match holder and striker, c.1935, $250-350.

CHESTERFIELD
Vigny
JACK
JUNIOR

A MAGNIFICENT collection of Baccarat glass perfume bottles and atomizers. Their colors are spectacular and this arrangement in ascending order by size shows them to their maximum advantage.

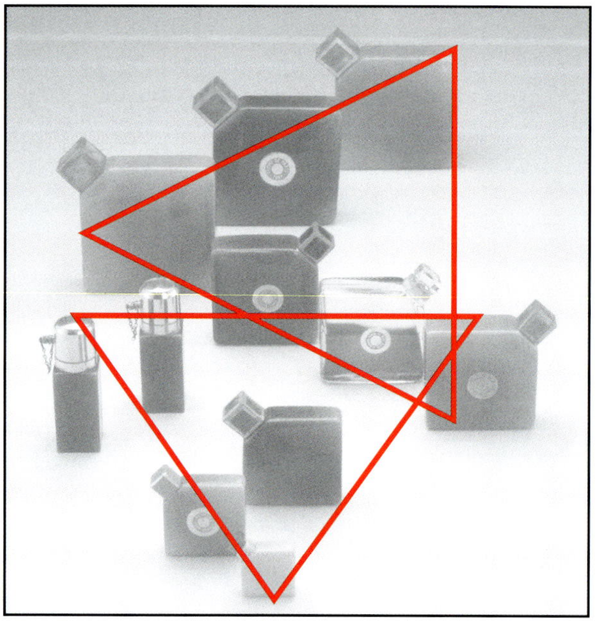

French Baccarat cased crystal perfume bottles for The House of Ybry from the thirties. They range in price from $2500, for the large size, to $600 for the smallest. The two upright atomizers are priced at $900-1000 each.

FEMME DE PARIS
YBRY
DEVINEZ
YBRY·PARIS

THREE DECADES of artist designed French perfume bottles. From the exquisite enamelling to the fine gilding, this group truly represents some of the icons of the perfume bottle design, whether it be in glass or ceramic.

From front: French Coeur en Folie by Rosine perfume bottle, c.1939, $3950-4250. Second row, from left: French Le Debut Noir powder compact and box by Richard Hudnut, c.1930, $225-275. Italian Egizia perfume bottle by La Ducale, c.1953, $2475-2525. French Rosine perfume bottle with tassel, c.1925, $1950-2050. French Depinoix Glassworks perfume bottle, c.1925, $950-1050. Back row, fom left: French Caresse Parisian perfume bottle by Guyla, c.1930, $5750-6000 with box. French Arlequinade perfume bottle by Paul Poiret for Rosine, c.1925, $7750-8000 with box. French Tuvach ZeZan perfume bottle, c.1940, $2400-2600. French Le Roi Soleil perfume bottle by Schiaparelli, c.1946, $14,500-15,500 with box.

BOMBS AND rockets from four decades form the theme for this grouping. All are table lighters save for the large silver plated rocket to the right of the group, which is a cocktail shaker.

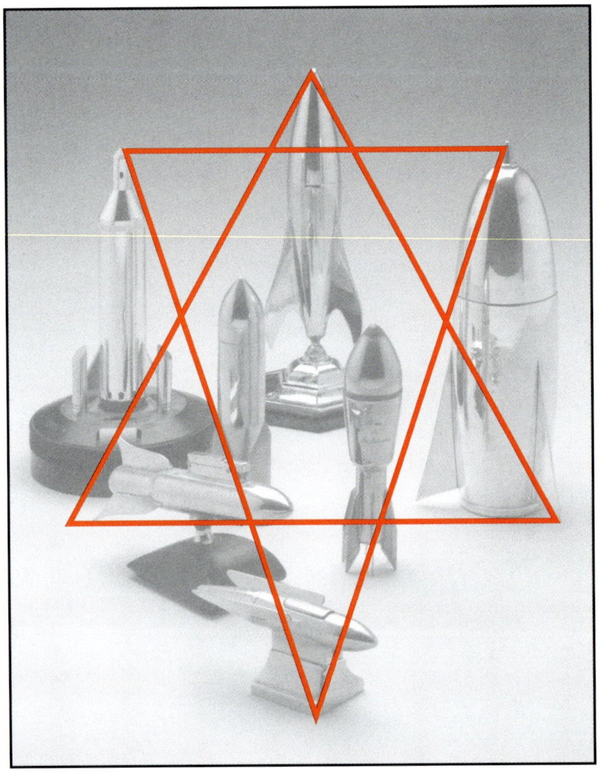

Clockwise from center: Japanese unmarked chrome wheel and flint torpedo table lighter, c.1939, $175-200. Japanese unmarked chrome and wood wheel and flint bomb table lighter, c.1939, $250-275. English unmarked wheel and flint bomb table lighter, c.1940, $250-275. Japanese Bronica electric rocket table lighter, c.1965, $175-200. English Planet chrome and Bakelite wheel and flint table lighter, c.1935, $250-275. German unmarked rocket cocktail shaker, c.1935, $600-700. Spanish unmarked mortar shell wheel and flint table lighter, c.1937, $175-250.

ART DEC

SCAPES

THE PRACTICE

A MASSIVE painting of the Florida Keys by Canadian painter David Allan Barr from 1956 is centred on this large Belgian Macassar Ebony veneered buffet. A collection of American tea and coffee sets is symmetrically displayed on the top surface and the whole grouping is bounded on either side by a pair of American brushed chrome torchiers.

Pair of American unmarked torchieres, c.1939, $3000-3750. Belgian unmarked Macassar Ebony buffet, c.1939, $9000-10,000. American Chase and Manning Bowman tea and coffee sets, c.1935-1955, $350-850 each.

THIS CANADIAN plaster faux fireplace and mantle is flanked by two American chrome and glass torchiers and topped by a wonderfully eccentric pearlized plaster Australian figural mantle clock. Two powder coated American tubular chairs are fronted by a chrome, glass and Lucite coffee table that is in turn placed on a hand knotted abstract rug of the 50's.

Canadian unmarked plaster faux fireplace, c.1925, $750-850. Canadian Hobbs Glass peach and white geometric mirror, c.1935, $850-950. Australian Westclox plaster figural nude mantle clock, c.1935, $520-625. American Bruce Hunt eight piece Bakelite and chrome cocktail set, c.1938, $650-750.

PEACH MIRRORED glass adds a touch of Hollywood glamour to this hallway. The hexagonal English Clark table displays an English cigarette box, Czechoslovakian perfume bottles, Canadian candleholders, plus a French Machine Age lamp and picture frame. An English peach mirror fronted wall clock hangs below a circular American mirror also in peach. Through the archway, we see into the living room where French and American club chairs in buff leather and faux leopard work together tonally to create a cohesive whole.

Pair of English Kaymet anodized aluminum vases, c.1945, $700-800. Danish L. Hjorth terra-cotta Aphrodite statue, c.1938, $2500-3000. French JAZ wood mechanical wall clock, c.1939, $450-550. Canadian Palatial Furniture Marquetry veneer armoir, c.1938, $900-1000. French brushed aluminum wall sconce, c.1935, $300-400.

EARTHTONES AND gold work in harmony in this grouping in an apartment entrance hallway. Sitting on an American Art Deco armoire, the two iconic English anodized aluminum Kaymet vases are balanced by the Danish water carrier ceramic sculpture. The French JAZ wall clock tones in with the pair of wood and chrome candleholders, also from France. Three anodized Japanese table lighters pick up the overall color scheme while a French brushed aluminum, glass and brass wall sconce tops the arrangement.

A LARGE FRENCH three-panel painted screen depicting Josephine Baker dancing at the Revenue Negre in Paris and painted by Floreal in 1925 provides a colorful backdrop to the small polychrome wooden Canadian table that displays Belgian ashtrays, American chrome Chase candleholders, an English Smiths clock, together with a Canadian Electrolier table lamp. Two American chrome and black chairs neatly bookend the total arrangement.

Canadian unmarked polychrome wood table, c.1935, $400-500. English Smiths mechanical table clock, c.1939, $275-325. Canadian Electrolier table lamp, c.1932, $1000-1500. Pair of Belgian unmarked chrome ball ashtrays, c.1935, $275-325 each. Pair of American unmarked chrome and leather chairs, c.1939, $350-400 each.

ONE FROM A pair of original framed 'Cartoons' for a stained glass window in All Hallows Church, St. Pancrass in London, England, provides a backdrop for this American Japanese black lacquer table from the 40's. The American color co-ordinated Machine Age torchiere and table lamp illuminate the pair of English photo frames and candleholders that are fronted in turn by two ultra Machine Age silver plated Japanese bud vases. The grouping is completed by a classic MacDermott brushed aluminum and black lacquer Machine Age magazine rack from Canada.

American unmarked bronzed metal and chrome torchiere, c.1935, $1350-1550. American unmarked bronzed metal and chrome table lamp with parchment shade, c.1940, $525-575. Pair of English unmarked tilt photo-frames, c.1935, $750-950. Pair of English unmarked chrome candlesticks, c.1935, $325-375. Pair of Japanese unmarked bud vases, c.1939, $295-350. Canadian MacDermott magazine rack, c.1945, $325-375.

LOVERS AND OTHER STRANGERS PAINTINGS BY JACK VETTRIANO
furniture & interiors
TERENCE CONRAN'S HOUSE BOOK
HOME in the Twenties and Thirties
DECORATIVE ART 1941 THE STUDIO YEAR BOOK
TWENTIETH-CENTURY ORNAMENT
DIVINELY

SCRAMBLE!

A small squadron consisting of two lamps, two chrome table lighters, a paperweight and an ashtray take off into the wide blue yonder, from an extreme Machine Age fan table in this aviation inspired grouping. The vertical lines in the pair of French industrial aluminum chairs contrast nicely with the horizontal bands of the fan housing of the table, whilst the early aviation poster introduces a strong note of both color and continuity to this grouping. As for the seemingly random positioning of the floor standing ashtray it is in actual fact linked to the rest of the items owing to a shared flight path with the other airplanes.

Right: Pair of unsigned French aluminum chairs, c.1935, $800. American "Kisco" fan table, c.1942, $1250. English Great Northern Railway First Aviation Races poster, c.1909, $2500. Canadian aluminum floor standing ashtray, c.1940, $1500.
On table from left: English aluminum, unsigned DH88 Comet paperweight, c.1934, $350. American cobalt blue glass and chrome airplane desk lamp, by Ray Schoeber for Premium Products, c.1940, $1750. American outsider art chrome flying boat lamp, c.1939. English jet plane table lighter by Dunhill, c.1958, and American airplane table lighter by Hamilton, c.1940, $175.

G. N. R.
ENGLAND'S FIRST AVIATION RACES
AT
DONCASTER
OCTOBER 15TH TO 23RD
SEE SPECIAL PROGRAMMES FOR TRAIN SERVICE & EXCURSION
ARRANGEMENTS GRATIS AT ANY GREAT NORTHERN OFFICE

THIS GUEST ROOM features a French twin bed bedroom suite, here accessorized with one of a pair of Canadian polychrome tables. Three pyrographic wood and applied brass screens by J.O. Gadoury decorate the wall while an adjustable chrome reading lamp is hung below a plaster and chrome illuminated wall mask. An American Machine Age centre lamp throws light on a vintage Indian bedspread.

American unmarked frosted glass chandelier, c.1940, $550-650. English unmarked chrome adjustable wall light, c.1925, $375-475. American unmarked back lit wall mask, c.1930, $300-375. Set of three Canadian J. O. Gadoury wooden pyrography and brass wall panels, c.1935, $5000-6000.

THIS HIGHLY symmetrical arrangement stands on a deep window sill. A Royalchrome table holds two Art Deco picture frames and a 50's lamp, while a small English chrome fireplace companion set stands in the middle. The large vases holding the calla lilies were actually the bases for floor standing ashtrays from the 40's in an earlier life.

Canadian Royalchrome Bakelite and chrome side table, c.1939, $425-450. Pair of American unmarked chrome skyscraper photo-frames, c.1935, $475-575. Canadian unmarked wood and brass lamp with parchment shade, c.1950, $375-425. English unmarked chrome companion set, c.1936, $250-295. Pair of American Chase Globe ash receivers, c.1936, $225-250. English unmarked candlesticks, c.1935, $175-200.

American unmarked figural male and female nude torchiere, c.1947, $1750-2000. Pair of French unmarked dance and music spelter figures with Bakelite cases, c.1929, $450-500. Czechoslovakian unmarked seven piece crystal liquere, c.1930, $750-850. Large French tri-color marble photo-frame, c.1925, $350-375. Pair of English unmarked Lotte Reiniger Dutch boy and girl silhouette candlesticks, c.1935, $250-300.

A PICTURE of the owners' two daughters in an Art Deco frame and surrounded by statuettes of other beauties and other items from an earlier age. The Arts and Craft chair to the left is balanced on the other side by a spectacular American figural torchiere with a swirled frosted glass shade that dates from the 40's.

The Savoy Cocktail Book

Top: English unmarked chrome vanity set, c.1930, $395-450. Pair of American unmarked figural boudoir lamps, c.1935, $650-750. English unmarked chrome cheval glass, c.1930, $750-850. Canadian unmarked cigarette box, c.1939, $125-150.

Bottom: American MAR-LE photo jewel box, c.1930, $275-325. American unmarked chrome table lamp, c.1935, $675-750. Pair of English unmarked cocktail shaker vases, c.1930, $125-150 each. German unmarked chrome mechanical table clock, c.1935, $275-325.

CHROME ART DECO items are beautifully displayed in this richly painted gabled guest room. On the vanity an English cheval-glass mirror reflects the geometric chrome brush and mirror set while a pair of American boudoir lights illuminate the surface. On the bedside table a chrome table lamp together with two English cocktail shaker vases stand next to a German alarm clock and a Mar-le jewellery box.

American unmarked center light, c.1932, $5500-6500. Belgian unmarked buffet/ china cabinet with copper and chrome accents, c.1935, $8500-9500. French unmarked lacquer dining table, c.1930, $5000-6000. Set of three Canadian J. O. Gadoury wooden pyrography and brass wall panels, c.1935, $5000-6000. Pair of Belgian unmarked chrome and wood triple candle hokders, c.1933, $300-400.

A LARGE Belgian asymmetrical glass fronted buffet stands under a three panel pyrographic screen from Canada. A dominant American Machine Age hanging light illuminates both the black lacquer dining table and the collection of framed Art Deco Spanish interior design prints on the right.

THIS ICONIC rocket-ship bar designed by the renowned English cabinet maker, Maurice Adams is here topped with a pair of French Bakelite table lamps, a French wrought iron mantle clock, and a collection of Danish Art Deco wooden frames, while centred on the floor stands an

English unmarked nickel plated adjustable doctor's lamp, c.1930, $850-950. Canadian unmarked anodized aluminum tea trolley, c.1945, $350-450. American Farber Bubble eight piece cocktail set, c.1937, $1250-1350. American Hotpoint four piece Bakelite and chrome coffee service, c.1939, $475-575. American unmarked chrome and red Bakelite tray, c.1936, $475-525. American Revere chrome and Bakelite magazine rack, c.1936, $375-475.

A NICKEL plated doctor's lamp stands ready to illuminate an Art Deco bar cart holding a large color co-odinated display of chrome and red Bakelite accented party items. On the wall, two original art photographic prints are framed in vintage frames while a Bakelite and chrome Revere magazine rack stands on the floor to the right.

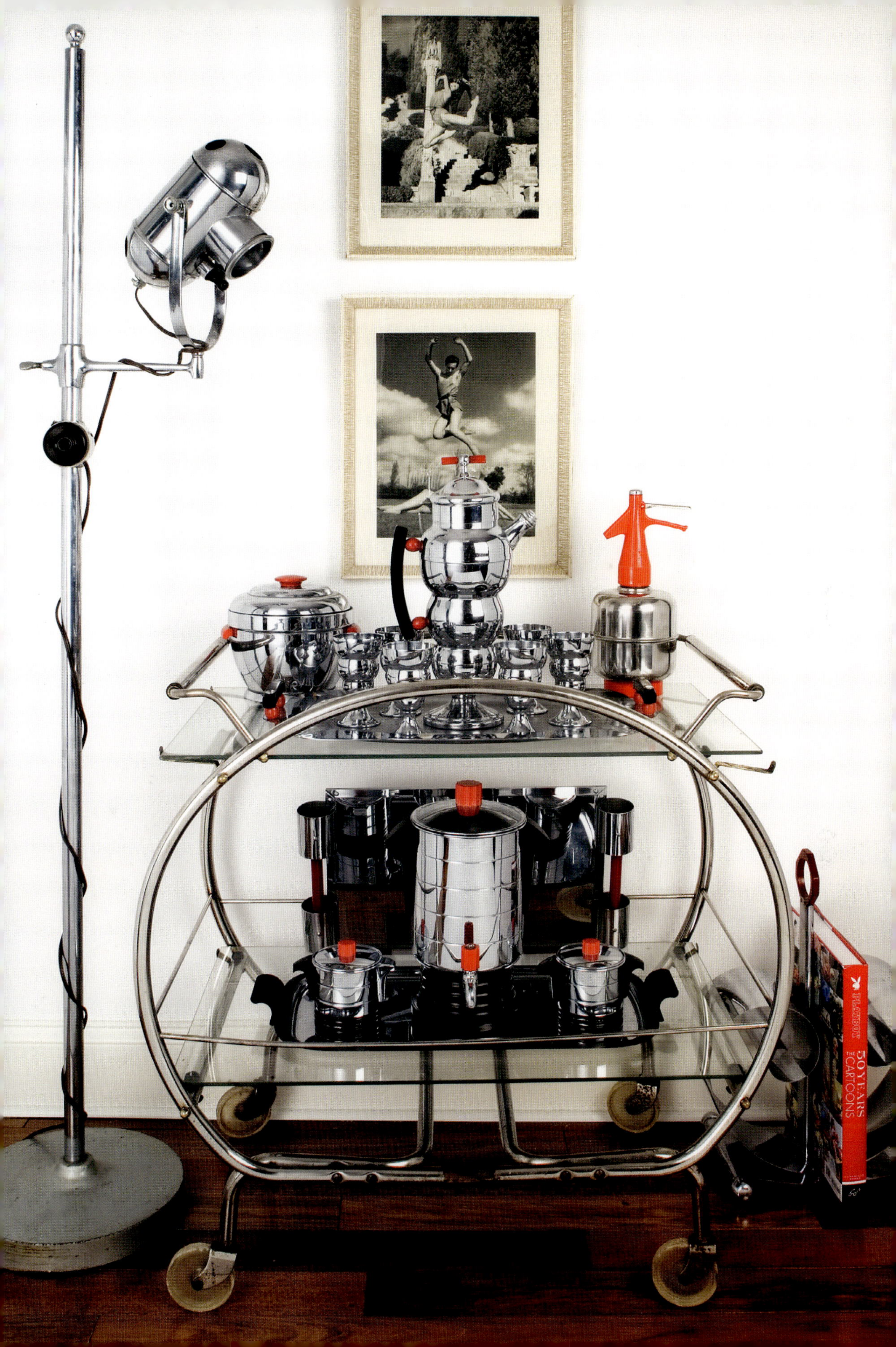
PLAYBOY
50 YEARS
THE CARTOONS

French unmarked wrought iron torchiere, c.1929, $1750-2000. American unmarked chrome and black lacquer side table, c.1935, $950-1050. English unmarked blonde wood cocktail bar with Bakelite accents, c.1935, $6500-7500. Pair of English Maurice Adams side chairs, c.1935, $3500-4000 each.

O N THE TOP surface of the large blonde wood bar stands a collection of black glass vases that serves to frame a French craquelure ceramic animal statue. In the foreground are two chairs by Maurice Adams with a chrome and black table and a magnificent French wrought iron lamp standing between them.

A SUSIE COOPER banded Kestrel coffee set is arranged on a wonderfully designed Machine Age convertible coffee table bar in front of an English Maurice Adams sofa. An Art Deco skyscraper bookcase in the rear displays a collection of both vintage and modern items while contemporary portraits hang on the wall.

English Susie Cooper banded Kestrel part coffee service, c.1936, $550-650. English unmarked wood and aluminum coffee/bar tray table, c.1935, $850-950. English Maurice Adams three seater couch, c.1935, $8500-9500. American unmarked skyscraper bookcase, c.1933, $1000-1250.

A MAGNIFICENT English grandfather clock stands behind a French dining table and chairs that is set for tea with a set of English Art Deco cups. The contemporary painting is paired with a modern vase in the centre of the table and a French Art Deco bronzed metal fountain chandelier hangs from above.

English unmarked oak mechanical pendulum grandfather clock, c.1929, $2000-2500. French unmarked seven piece dining room suite, c.1929, $4500-5000. French unmarked bronzed metal and frosted glass waterfall chandelier, c.1935, $2750-3000. English Shelley part tea service, c.1939, $250-300.

THIS CHEERFULLY designed English dinner service was a gift to the present owner's parents on the occasion of their marriage in 1940. It is now proudly displayed in the summer kitchen and only brought out for very special occasions.

English Burleigh Ware, handpainted part dinner service, c.1937. These pieces range in price from $35 to $250.

THE PONY SKIN rug sets the palette for this fireplace grouping that combines both contemporary and vintage pieces. Two American tubular chrome chairs frame a contemporary coffee table and mantle piece, both decorated with vintage ceramics, while two American Art Deco wall sconces bookend a Canadian oil pastel landscape.

Pair of American Wolfgang Hoffman tubular chrome chairs, c.1935, $950-1050. Pair of American unmarked chrome and milk glass wall sconces, c.1935, $450-550. English thirties Beswick Vases, $150-300 each.

A COLLECTION of English Beswick ceramics is arranged on a contemporary modern glass topped iron coffee table and an American cabinet from the 40's, that in turn stands below a period figure painting in oils. An American tubular chrome arm chair has been newly upholstered in a cheerful contemporary fabric that fits perfectly in this sunny room.

American unmarked Art Moderne buffet, c.1944, $950-1250. American unmarked tubular chrome and wood upholstered chair, c.1939, $750-850. American Chase Continental four piece coffe service, c.1936, $500-600. Pair of English Beswick twin candleholders, c.1938, $200-250. English thirties Beswick multi-color glaze pieces on coffee table by Owen, $150-400.

A GILBERT Rohde suite is matched with contemporary in this dramatic bedroom. The American designer theme is enhanced with the Herman Miller clock by Rohde on the desk and the Henry Dreyfuss Thermos jug and tray beside the bed.

American Gilbert Rohde bedroom suite, c.1936, $7000-10,000. American Herman Miller mechanical desk clock by Gilbert Rohde, c.1936, $650-750. American Henry Dreyfuss brown Thermos carafe set, c.1938, $350-450. Canadian Hobbs Glass bevelled and deckle edged circular mirror, c.1939, $550-650.

BELGIAN RAILWAYS
CENTENARY OF THE INDEPENDENCE OF BELGIUM
LIEGE 1930
INTERNATIONAL EXHIBITION
APRIL
NOV.
INDUSTRY
PURE AND APPLIED SCIENCE
ANCIENT WALLOON ART

A VERY effective tri-angulated display of classic English Beswick matte honeyglazed ceramics, in which the stark monochromatic style just serves to heighten the extraordinary Art Deco design of this pottery.

English thirties Beswick jug, vase, wall mask and wall pocket collection. Many of the best of these were designed by Owen and they range in price from $200-500.

A HALFRED Tygesen pastel winter landscape from the 40's is placed between two flamboyantly carved American console lamps on an Art Deco bookcase filled with design reference books. A Royalchrome table with a vintage phone stands within easy reach of an iconic Kem Weber chrome and black leather chair.

American Lloyd chrome and leather armchair by Kem Weber, c.1937, $6000-7000. Pair of American unmarked, hand carved free form console lamps, c.1945, $700-800. American Royalchrome two tiered Bakelite and chrome table, c.1936, $450-550. Collection of thirties monochromatic English Beswick vases, $100-250.

Essential ART DECO
ART DECO NEW YORK
Art Deco Interiors
AMERICAN ART DECO
TASCHEN

THIS BAKELITE and chrome accented chest of drawers is part of a four piece American bedroom suite from the 30's. One of a pair of Oriental style table lamps, and complementary styled period hanging mirror together with a Machine Age style clock and a tonally appropriate grouping of ceramics complete the arrangement for a guest room.

THE RICH COLOR of this Heywood Wakefield buffet serves as an ideal display area for both Beswick china and a contemporary Oriental lamp, while three Tygesen oil pastels are arranged on the wall and frame the overall arrangement perfectly.

American Heywood Wakefield eight piece dining room suite, c.1947, $3500-4500. Collection of thirties English Beswick jugs and vases, $150-250. Canadian Halfred Tygesen oil pastel landscapes and seascapes with original frames, c.1940, $350-450.

Italian unmarked mirror lined Futurist bar, c.1939, $9000-10,000. Canadian Eclipse Fountain Pens chrome and neon electric advertising clock, c.1930, $2500-3000. American unmarked spun aluminum table torchieres, c.1939, $2000-3000. Canadian unmarked etched glass wall mirror, c.1945, $650-750. English Teddy Tail and Friends children's rug, c.1935, $750-850.

A COLLECTION of French Faience ceramics from Provence is housed in and on a magnificant Italian Futurist bar. Two massive table torchieres flank a large chrome neon advertising clock. The children's rug in front of the bar depicts Teddy Tail and Friends, who were arguably some of the most popular cartoon figures in Britain during the thirties.

ECLIPSE
FOUNTAIN PENS
"Make You Write Better"

French unmarked office dresser with chrome accents, c.1935, $2750-3750. Canadian Richard Hudnut point of sale triptych, c.1926, $500-600. On top surface of credenza from left: French Lalique Plate, c.1932, $500-600. French Lalique Eagles' Head radiator mascot, c.1939, $4000-4500. French Lalique Flausa for Roget et Gallet perfume bottle, c.1914, $4000-5000. Large French Lalique Deux Figurines mechanical illuminated clock, c.1929, $23,000-23,500. French Lalique Quatre Perruches mechanical clock, c.1920, $500-5500. French Lalique plate, c.1930, $500-600. French Lalique Spirit of The Wind Radiator mascot, c.1928, $30,000-35,000. French Lalique Deux Figurines perfume bottle, c.1929, $2000-2500. American Belmet Products Rollaround ashtray, c.1939, $450-550.

SOME STUNNING examples of the glass of René Lalique adorn this credenza that is in fact just part of a large suite of French Art Deco office furniture. Above it is a point of sale card triptych, advertising the perfumes of Richard Hudnut. In front an American Rollabout ashtray stands next to a classic Marcel Bruer designed leather and chrome chair

Three Flowers Creams
CLEANSING CREAM
"Thoroughly cleanses each tiny pore"
VANISHING CREAM
"Insures adherence of face powder"
SKIN and TISSUE CREAM
"Protects delicate skin tissues"
RICHARD HUDNUT

THE STAIR RAIL in this photograph was in fact installed in the 50's but its Art Deco styling fits perfectly with the original Cabaret posters from Paris in the 20's. The metal and wood Art Nouveau table on the landing displays a small and colorful grouping of English Rouge Royale china.

French unmarked Art Nouveau metal and wood table, c.1905, $500-750. French Caron/M. Ducelier Josephine Baker poster, c.1950, $1000-1250. French unmarked cocktail poster, c.1938, $650-700. English Carlton Ware, Rouge Royale plate, c.1936, $100-150. English Carlton Ware, Rouge Royale vase, c.1936, $400-450. English Carlton Ware, Rouge Royale double handled sugar bowl, c.1936, $125-150. English Carlton Ware, Rouge Royale cup and saucer, c.1936, $50-75.

JOSEPHINE
le 12 FÉVRIER
1927
AU
BAL
NEGRE
BAR

TWO MASSIVE Art Deco department store chrome display shelves are placed together in order to display a very impressive collection of cocktail shakers. They range from very valuable examples from the 20's to the more accessible examples from the 50's, and when they are all grouped together they form a very interesting focal point for this large contemporary kitchen.

Pair of American unmarked chrome department store shelves, c.1939, $3000-4000. French Courtois poster for Champagne Roger Desivry, c.1935, $2250-2750. The cocktail shakers come from various coun-

PAGNE
SIVRY

china from the thirties ranges in price from around $40 for the smaller pieces up to $800 for some of the larger pieces on the top shelf.

D ISPLAYED on the French dining table is part of a Clarice Cliff Biarritz dinner service while on the buffet and small glass table are displayed groupings of English china by Shelly and Carlton Ware. The wall sized contemporary painting in the background suggests the color scheme for the upholstery of the dining chairs.

French unmarked eight piece dining suite, c.1935, $8000-9000. English Clarice Cliff twenty four piece Biarritz dinner service, c.1939, $1500-1750. English green Carlton Ware tea set, c.1936, $500-600. English Shelley part tea service, c.1940, $600-700.

Canadian unmarked tri-color wood vanity, c.1936, $1750-2250. English unmarked drum storage vanity stool, c.1935, $450-550. American unmarked chrome torchiere, c.1936, $1500-1600. American unmarked tortoise shell Lucite purse, c.1949, $300-350. American unmarked chrome table lamp, c.1935, $650-750. German unmarked chrome mechanical desk clock, c.1936, $275-325. American unmarked three tiered aluminum and glass hanging lamp, c.1942, $1750-2000.

IN THIS BEDROOM a mirrored vanity that was custom built in the 30's for one of the suites in the Park Plaza Hotel, Toronto, Canada, reflects a huge French grand lit bed with built in bedside tables. Also reflected is a three tier American Machine Age glass and aluminum hanging light and a massive circular mirror with Lucite accents

A LARGE Belgian nickel mounted Palissander glass fronted buffet houses a collection of brightly colored French Faience. On top, a pair of hand carved Heifitz bird lamps guard a statue depicting two swimming men that in turn sits in front of a large etched floral mirror. Two faux leopard skin covered club chairs face each other across a glass topped coffee table on which stands a Belgian crystal vase.

Belgian unmarked Palissander glass fronted china cabinet/buffet with nickel accents, c.1930, $9000-10,000. Pair of American Heifitz figural bird console lamps, c.1942, $2500-3000. Pair of French unmarked burl wood veneer club chairs, c.1933, $4000-4500. American unmarked brushed aluminum and wood torchiere with fiberglass shade, c.1945, $1500-1750.

AN AMERICAN telephone table from the 40's is illuminated by a streamlined Canadian chrome and wood floor lamp with a two tiered parchment shade and a strip light chrome and glass sconce. Above the table an American hand colored polo print by Sue is displayed in a signed National Recovery Act chrome frame and tones in perfectly with the other chrome and bronze items on the surface of the table.

American unmarked telephone table and stool combination, c.1939, $950-1250. American unmarked chrome and glass wall sconce, c.1936, $250-300. American unmarked chrome and wood streamline floor lamp, c.1947, $850-950. American unmarked chrome and bronzed metal desk lamp, c.1935, $350-400. American polo block print by Sue in National Recovery Act chrome frame, c.1936, $275-325.

NORTHUMBERLAND 2006
AUTO ACCIDENT?

THE FOSTED GLASS circle on the Machine Age light fitting is replicated in the lines of the large circular mirror in this bathroom. In the reflection we can see a 60's American lamp standing on an Art Deco black lacquer cabinet beneath a French Bakelite wall clock. An English plaster nude statuette holds centre stage on the mirror shelf together with a Japanese ceramic girl's head and a pair of Bakelite and chrome candleholders.

American unmarked twin bulb wall sconce, c.1939, $300-325. Canadian unmarked circular wall mirror with blonde wood shelf, c.1969, $350-450. English unmarked girl on a globe plaster statuette, c.1939, $250-300. Pair of English unmarked candlesticks, c.1935, $200-275. Japanese unmarked ceramic girl's head, c.1945, $175-225.

Pair of English/American Emor Globe radios, c.1946, $1500-1750 each. American unmarked reverse painted electric wall clock, c.1939, $350-400. German unmarked chrome and mirror two tiered sleigh table, c.1936, $850-950. Canadian Outsider Art aluminum and Lucite twin plane lamp, c.1945, $650-700. American Evercraft ten piece cocktail set, c.1938, $700-800. French aluminum and glass wall sconce, c.1929, $475-525.

ELECTRONIC

A HIGH ART Deco hall table and cupboard unit displays just part of a magnificent collection of René Lalique glass items. Four hood ornaments and two small vases stand grouped on either side of a magnificent Serpent vase that in turn links tonally with the painting above.

French unmarked hall table/cupboard, c.1929, $3000-4000. French Lalique Serpent vase, c.1925, $22,500-27,500. On left: French Lalique Falcon radiator mascot, c.1925, $3750-4250. French Lalique Dragonfly radiator mascot, c.1928, $6250-6750. French Lalique Coq et Plumes vase, c.1928, $850-1250. On right: French Lalique Five Horses radiator mascot, c.1925, $7750-8250. French Lalique Boar radiator mascot, c. 1929, $2750-3250. French Lalique Mosaic vase in pale amber, c.1927, $1750-2000